NO REDACTIONS

D. E. RITTERBUSCH

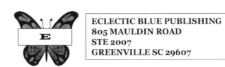

ECLECTIC BLUE PUBLISHING
805 MAULDIN ROAD
STE 2007
GREENVILLE SC 29607

2024

ECLECTIC BLUE PUBLISHING
805 MAULDIN ROAD
STE 2007
GREENVILLE SC 29607

EclecticBluePublishing@gmail.com
423-202-0937

One of the great literary changes that has transpired in my lifetime is a cross-genre realization—how prose poems blend seamlessly into flash fiction, flash fiction into straight fiction, straight fiction into creative non-fiction and the literary essay. The old constraints have been lifted; the taboos no longer sacred. There are resistors, of course, but the pleasures of this change are considerable.

D.E.R.

For those few and lonely readers who over the many years have appreciated my work.

ALSO BY D. E. RITTERBUSCH

LESSONS LEARNED: POETRY OF THE VIETNAM WAR & ITS AFTERMATH

FAR FROM THE TEMPLE OF HEAVEN

TIPPING POINT (DANCING ON THE)

THE STINGER

A NOTE ON THE DOOR

FUBAR & CO. (forthcoming)

ACKNOWLEDGMENTS

AETHLON: THE JOURNAL OF SPORT LITERATURE: *Everything in Black and White*

DEADLY WRITER'S PATROL: *Bullet Eater*

CIGALE LITERARY MAGAZINE: *China Green*

ONE PERSON'S TRASH: *Living in the Apartment Above the Liquor Store*

REVUE LISA/LISA e-journal: *A Mathematical Geography*

SCAPEGOAT REVIEW: *Psych Test*

WAR, LITERATURE & the ARTS JOURNAL: *A Mathematical Geography; After Shakespeare's When Icicles Hang by the Wall; Soul-Stinger*

NO REDACTIONS
TABLE OF CONTENTS

SUBWAY BUSKER

His guitar case holds a few dollars, mostly small change, but a couple of five-dollar bills. It is cool near the tunnel, and the subway tile echoes a bit. His song is lost as a train hurtles by. If this is living for one's art that's fine, admirable in a way, sad in another. I watch a couple of passersby drop a few coins, but most are oblivious, not that they don't care, but caring is exhausting—let the upper crust, the highest echelons of society, those who have money, let them support the arts. Comically, revelatory to but a few, we are all buskers, all playing the instruments of our lives, almost always out of tune, almost always drowned-out by the trains or whatever passes us by.

THE NATURE OF IRREVERSIBILITY

Three blocks away, nearing midnight, the delivery boy was shot before he delivered the pizza. The cops all asked the same question: why didn't the robber wait until after delivery to increase his take? All he got was a few dollars and change. But not many people pay cash even for a pizza these days; credit cards are safer, so few carry cash, and why didn't the robber know this? You know this. Your grandmother knows this. Such is the failure of our educational system. Isn't it time we spent less time memorizing the school song, a requirement for graduation, and taught simple everyday life-affirming facts just like this one, demonstrated in a pool of blood around the boy: those who deliver don't carry much cash. The body lying in its chalk marks is getting colder, the policewoman is shivering, red and blue lights rake a cool breeze across our cheeks and those of our neighbors. Even in its thermal blanket, the pizza is getting cold, a fundamental law of thermodynamics all cops and robbers should know.

REVEILLE

Reveille and out of the barracks before dawn, standing in formation, at attention, then at ease as our platoon sergeant offers in his stentorian voice a few matutinal instructions before chow. I look up at the beautiful dark night, this hour before dawn, meteors streaming across the sky, a cosmic celebration. Later, after a barracks inspection, SSGT Trutt raked our balls over the coals for our failure to make bunks tight enough to bounce a bowling ball, one of many gigs the platoon was given. A butt can had a butt stuck to the bottom of that can and a shaving brush found wet. I wondered whose it was; no one ever used them; they were for display purposes only. To this very day I have one on display in my upstairs bath, a reminder of my military days. Sarge continued bellowing: "And one of you idiots was looking at the stars this morning while in formation, not paying attention as usual. You're in the Army. Pay attention goddam it or you'll end up dead. It's the little details you don't pay attention to that will kill you— get with the program." I smiled, knowing that idiot was me, and that morning meteor shower such a fine and splendid detail it could always save my life.

THE GOOD LIFE

This is a day, a time of life, when one asks, "What the hell just happened?" oblivious to most everything now that nothing matters—too old, too jaded, too circumspect for love, war, any passion left in the world or even a good wine that no longer facilitates conversation, but instead, gives rise to sleep, perchance to dream—Ha! Fat chance; dreams left long ago, no fantasies, no hardening recollections. Remember that witty girl who, when the music ran down, said, "Let's put on something soft and sexy" and jumped onto the stereo cabinet and lifted her skirt. Well, that's never going to happen again now that music plays from a smart phone or from Alexa, a woman who undoubtedly undresses in the dark, whose husband has never seen her naked—just ask that repressed woman for *Carmina Burana* and see what you get: sound quality of a meat grinder and an abbreviated rendition that embarrasses the entirety of the universe. Reminds me of the time I was conversing with a woman I hardly knew, discussing some matter of literary history, a penetrating and enlivened conversation, and she reached up my shorts, pulled out my thing and said, "I like the shape of your penis." If that is the only thing I take to my grave, I will live and die happy, though happiness may be overrated. A friend— she's been known to know things— once said, "It doesn't take much to make a middle-aged man happy," a revelatory insight worthy of the Worthies. Come here; this is a morning to dance around the living room until, exhausted, I just hang on to you, your body pressed close, Rodrigo's *Concierto de Aranjuez* playing in the parlor, dancing heavily until we fall down drunk on each others' exhalations, my hand finding its way under your flowery blouse.

THE PERILS of LEARNING SCIENCE in AMERICA

A cop stops Jim for speeding. He raps his knuckles on the window, and Jim rolls it down. "License and registration." Jim fumbles. "Do you know the speed limit?" the cop asks, his hand loosely on the grip of his revolver. "186,000 miles per second," Jim replies, "or roughly 670 million mph." Two shots and Jim didn't need to produce his insurance card.

Perhaps this is merely a variation on an old joke. Perhaps. But with scientific literacy declining, with so many NBA players saying the earth is flat, with so many climate change deniers, with so many believing the sun revolves around the earth, with so many disbelieving in the fundamental laws of biological evolution and refusing vaccinations, a recent survey has demonstrated that only 26% of the nation's population get the above joke, and the percentage is projected to decline yearly with a declination angle greater than the steep and proverbial slippery slope so much alluded to in our political discourse.

What went so very wrong in a world where many of us learned that dinosaurs once thrived in Montana, when so many of us made rockets out of tinfoil and match heads, when we saw the skewed tracks of particles through a cloud chamber, and we all built fizzy volcanoes to spew an ever-delightful mess in the first or second grade?

WATER BOATMAN

There is a beetle, a small beetle barely two millimeters in length, living in water, hanging upside down from a slender reed, and it sings with a stentorian voice, *lirico spinto*, singing the loudest song of any in the animal world relative to its size, nearly a hundred db. Only the blue whale with a resonant cavern for a throat can match that beetle's level of sound. Lover of *Moby Dick*, of whale music, I listen to records of their songs and rejoice in the opera of their lives. But this beetle, with a penis thinner than a strand of human hair, uses his penis to make one of the loudest sounds in all God's bestiary, stridulation an admirable evolutionary feat: his rigid penis rubs against his rock-hard abdomen, and the watery stage reverberates with his song. This is grand opera for the adulation of a mate. He sings to his prospective lover, desirous of a great love: Violetta and Alfredo, Tristan and Isolde, Aïda and Radamès. Surely there is an entomological lesson here; you may be thinking size, the answer to the age old trite and trivial question, but it is opera, the great arias and duets. Knowing all things are possible, all things achievable in this world, I am going to extend the evolutionary reach and teach my penis to sing.

WHY I HAVE NO SENSE OF HUMOR

I love Freon, more than any other halocarbon, a refrigerant so much responsible for cooling the planet, well sort of, in home air conditioners, automobiles, refrigerated trucks and freight cars: remember those sweltering days in a car hotter than the proverbial oven, or, given the inutility of that cliché, because it is a cliché, hot as an oiled, smoking, iron pan used to blacken redfish in New Orleans. That hot. Such heat unbearable even at highway speeds, windows open, wind noise tearing at one's ears. Now A/C is standard, and those junkyard autos vent Freon into the atmosphere destroying the ozone layer. For every good there is an equal and opposite evil, a law Newton should have recorded. There is always a trade-off: keep the planet from assured destruction OR make love. Years ago, in an old hotel room in Sattahip, the woman I was with cried out, "I'm hot! I'm hot! And I thought she wanted to make love even harder, more ardor to swell the night, but O she was literal, that room—no air conditioning to cool things down, too hot even to make love, the atmosphere of Venus, literally.

And there are, or were before it was banned, other practical uses, not just in industry but in military applications as well—Freon soaked anti-personnel mines dropped from above along trails of infiltration, outside defensive perimeters. Freon evaporated, the mine is armed. Once a defense plant supervisor offered a demonstration designed to prove the safety of the Freon saturated mine filled with explosives: he whacked it with a broomstick and it exploded injuring himself and several workers at the plant.

And then there is the entertainment value of Freon, used to freeze a dead mouse then whacked with a hammer on the sidewalk, a demonstration of cryogenics to our testosterone driven minds. It shattered like the old high school chem lab experiment, the teacher dipping a rose or carnation in a container of liquid nitrogen and then smacking it theatrically on the soapstone countertop, breaking it into uncountable pieces to the delight of students everywhere.

I remember those gray pieces of mouse warming in the noonday sun, a spot of blood thawing.

There is no imagination now—none. Who would take a dead rodent, dip it in Freon captured from an old refrigerator and whack it with a ball peen hammer? What passes is simply transcription, vicarious veridical knowledge, verifiable, repeatable, a fact of scientific inquiry, knowledge gained from memorization or, even less, from Wikipedia tables and charts. But, what's lost in this, the wonder, the bloody truth, the uncorrupted beauty of Freon, and the shattered, flying chunks of mouse.

WINDOW DRESSING

Breath clouds the glass; the breather, a man with clumped strands of hair, looks into the window of an upscale department store. Mannequins stare into the vacuous space above his head as if searching for the vanishing point in a trompe l'oeil painting. The man uses his reflection to cut strand after oily strand, cocking his head, his breath occluding the features of his face, scissors at unnatural angles in his unpracticed hand. No one walking by wishes to see the fevered, concentrating look in his eyes, nor do they stop to look at the window display: beautiful men and women dressed beautifully and arranged with artistic, holiday flair. The man wears a worn Harris tweed jacket stretched out of shape, pocket flap torn and flapping, collar dirty and smudged. When new the jacket might have been worn long ago by some humanities professor who taught at a local college. Perhaps it had been worn by a businessman, a man used to navy or gray suits worn workdays throughout his years; jacketless he felt naked on weekends and wore the tweed on runs to the hardware store believing a man should be self-reliant and do his own repairs. It is the concept of repair we are considering here; repose and repair for the soul, a reworking of a sermon read last Sunday, part of a subscription service so the minister is freed from the tedium of writing during the week. *What Are the Responsibilities for Repair?* titles our sermon. Should the professor rework the syllabus for his course? Should students retake it now desirous to learn? Should only experts make repairs—a licensed plumber, a certified electrician? Should the minister write his own words, a trained barber administer last rites to the homeless man's hair, falling in the winter glint of scissors opening, closing, cutting.

A CANONICAL BETRAYAL

In the Gospel of Thomas, Jesus says women cannot enter into heaven, and just so, with errant theology rampant, Luther throws an inkwell across a frigid room aiming at the Devil, a bemused smirk blazoned on his face. Ink splatters on the wall like blood, yet the Devil holds his ground. He knows ink is not a threat no matter how well-written. Also thrown are various books of the Bible, leaving them for Catholics to restore, to defend, and the rest, a couple dozen in all, tossed and strewn, left for the righteous ones to be picked up like soft drink cans littered along a highway. There must be retrievals, defenses, consensus of the Canon. The Believers accept anything with authority. A uniform works best, some priestly garb to counter Luther naked in the cold walls striking himself repeatedly with a scourge, cleansing away evil, putting to death the sins of the flesh. Comically, the cosmic irony omnipresent like background radiation, so many Catholic treatises ridicule Luther for his exclusions ("straw not worthy to be burned"), considered theological whimsy, not realizing in the blinding light of scripture that their inclusions, their exclusions, are identical in end game effect. (I prefer the Popes [Leo X, Alexander VI] who rejoice at naked boys leaping out of cakes—so much honesty there, the practice bereft of hypocrisy.) Perhaps, like children fabricating sins for the Confessional, there is an inner drive to anger God at one's offense. I have known a minister of God curse his creator hour after endless hour shouting, blaspheming, crying a Calvinist sermon into the dark hours of a city night begging punishment, penance unlike Daniel— his various stories expunged—who subdued the wildness of the world, a wiser man than Solomon though his wisdom suffers from a morality of judgment, from jurisprudent logic and reason. O for the believers who accept the story of Susanna, the story of false witness, debauchery, lechery of the hierarchy, Rabbis old and ugly as their sin—how fitting is the cliché born of eternity. Mastic or oak and the lie is known. I wonder if the elders pleaded at their executions. Did they pray for forgiveness out of fear or genuine sorrow and remorse? Regardless, Susanna is always virtuous in her beauty and Artemisia captures her modest grace as she knew full well the lechery and lust of her father's friend, her tutor, her rapist. The sin of betrayal not codified. So the failure here is not that the story merely represents moral instruction, the wages of sin, a common parable of life's temptations, but that for this the story is not to be used for the formation of doctrine, doctrine separate from lessons of morality and of little value to the sermon or the faith. Should not the Rabbis—elderly, enlarged prostates, a time before Cialis—have been content to look, admiring Susanna's beauty from afar, behind mastic or oak, just as we admire her beauty displayed on luxuriant museum walls, recalling a time when such beauty was more than memory or lust. But the lesson, the moral consciousness divined from doctrine, is an inclusion in Daniel, in the Catholic Bible, the story of Susanna there for every priest and fatted Bishop to behold, and still that misbehavior of the Elders is embraced, made their very own, their hands groping in the choir. Rethink the Song of Solomon, wisest man who ever lived, who compared a woman's breasts to the twin fawns of a gazelle and, a passage later, to the clusters of a palm tree. Not content with the charms of a thousand wives he falls in love with a Shulamite, worshipper of Moloch and Remphan, but the bargain here an equal exchange of values, idol worship in exchange for sex. An easy sacrifice: five locusts crushed in Solomon's hand and her charms are his—Such foolish things men do for women. Thusly, Solomon's testament is scorned as if forgiveness were not virtue, his frailty, unable to exorcise his demons within, made fool by God, ridiculed by ignominious minions, he walks the streets mouthing gibberish: babble so often the end point of wisdom.

RANCH HAND

nly you can prevent a forest—the old joke about deforestation—Agent Orange, Agent Blue, and the joke told by those soldiers and Marines exposed—"I died in Vietnam and didn't even know it." Still, in the war museum, malformed fetuses in jars, the joke takes hold, and hare-lipped children have grown old, their faces staring back, mimicking the old refrain: Only you can—only you.

ANIMALS BOLT, BIRDS FLY AWAY

Animals bolt, birds fly away quickly as if by instinct when startled by someone's gaze, when they notice some predator, real or imagined, staring at them with concentrated attention. It is thought these creatures believe they are that voyeur's prey, that they are being stalked, hunted, the desired next meal for any carnivorous critter eyeing them. This is why women frown upon being looked at, even appreciatively, as such appreciation is similar to the admiration given to any exquisite repast by a venerator of gastronomical wizardry. I have known women who react with scorn when one's attention is drawn to a lettered T-shirt, some trite saying, philosophic or political, some shop-worn homily, some advertisement for Harleys or a particular designer in vogue (literally) at the moment. When one grows up in a literate atmosphere, devouring even the messages on cereal boxes, it is no wonder the attention given to the T-shirt: *John 3:16. Rolling Stones—The First Farewell Tour. The Brontes: A Literary Festival. I'm With Stupid*, an arrow pointing in an indiscriminate direction. "What do you think of the T-shirt," asks a female colleague of a male colleague wishing I suppose for some laudatory remark, praise for the artistry advertising that season's art festival. "I had not noticed," he says, "having been instructed long ago not to address my concentration on a woman's chest, no matter how well written, how well illustrated." Breast binding, like foot binding, should be the rule for women who do not wish to be recognized as women. Crossing one's arms across the chest, disguising the fact of breasts, merely calls attention to them. It is best to enact laws forbidding women to breast feed in public though most often the nipple is obscured by the sucking infant, such laws necessary lest civilization continue on this path to perdition. Still, impropriety is an acute manifestation of human behavior, and now even the *National Geographic* apologizes for those topless natives spanning their pages for decades. Can one even in mythological treatises mention the Amazon warriors who cut off a breast so that the bow string would not be mammarily impeded as the arrow left the bow? Once, on a third or fourth date, a young woman recently emigrated from Cuba where Marxism allows for topless beaches, asked, "Are you a breast man or a leg man?" "I love shoulders," I said, not elaborating further. A woman's shoulders are stunningly beautiful and defy the convention which is trite and demeaning. In this, I can rise above it all, because no woman cares that I keep my male gaze fixed upon her shoulders, no remonstrations, no frowning at the attention, and she is not wired to bolt or fly from my presence, my appreciations, and I may feast as if every day is a day of Thanksgiving. It may be the 21st century, but we are still in the dark ages, and there are no preparations for feminism in the 22nd based on recent political and legal arguments. For years I taught classes on censorship, the various shifts in time of what is considered risqué or obscene or acceptable according to current fashion: once dimpled knees were in, then they were out. Bridget Bardot, Jayne Mansfield, et al were in, then Twiggy and the anorexic fashion: Nothing tastes as good as skinny feels. I used the example of an English instructor who objected to a Goya painting hanging in her classroom, *The Naked Maja* of course, and the instructor was convinced male students paid more attention to the painting than to her literary insights. "Was this painting designed for the male gaze?" I asked my students. "No," a handsome young man with many girlfriends responded. "She's too fat." An honest if not aesthetically accurate assessment, and the number of his girlfriends suffered no depletion. Only weeks ago, civic minded teachers and administrators in a Florida high school doctored photos of female students who, being largely endowed, showed a bit of cleavage in their high school yearbooks; a black rectangle was posted over the offending cleavage and the girls appeared breastless. Body shaming de rigeur for Florida—but on the beach, in the college classrooms, girls wear bikinis so small as an old girlfriend said they covered as much as two Band-Aids and a cork. Surely that description is offensive if not especially odious yet, remember, a woman offered that description, and I lay no claim to it. Women may say such things; I certainly may not, nor would I, given my meditative appreciation of shoulders. Still, despite the prejudices, the hypocrisies, the patriarchal stereotypes, it has been good to see women of a different ilk: I used to teach how politics of the moment informed our behaviors including our senses of humor, how it was all right to laugh at dumb men jokes (Why is sperm white and urine yellow? So men can tell if they are coming or going), but not all right to laugh at dumb blond jokes, blonds a protected species (Why did the blond crawl over the chain link fence? To see what was on the other side). Usually, it was the blond women who laughed at those jokes regardless of the prohibition, women self-aware, self-assured, able to recognize the absurdity of those demeaning jokes and rise above them unaffected. Teaching John Donne's *Elegie: Going to Bed*, after playfully explicating *The Flea*, I read the lines: "License my roving hands and let them go/Before, behind, between, above, below./O my America! My new-found-land . . ." and a woman smiled so beautifully at these lines, showing such a wondrous shock of recognition at their compelling truth that I am sure I gave her an A just for her response, more truth there than in all the Holy Sonnets. Other women, in a class on obedience to authority, the rubric that defines our lives, told me of their embarrassment at being pulled aside by a teacher or principal on a hot day in high school for having straps on their blouses or dresses, spaghetti straps, not two fingers in width; perhaps my secret fetish is discovered, and my aesthetic proclivities are to be constrained, outlawed for degeneracy. Still, it is curious how young women are alternately ashamed or immensely proud of their bodies, their breasts, often the source of body shaming in our culture, these primary sexual characteristics thought to be often too large or too small—"More than a handful is wasted," I had learned from properly enculturated, chauvinistic classmates who had snapped the bra straps of young girls on the grade school playground during recess. Weirdly, in a most ironic way, where according to some feminist theory, women should be allowed to be women throwing off the shackles of a patriarchal society and not signing chastity pledges, so many women have embraced the censorious nature of cancel culture, reinforcing the old values, reminding women that they are women but they need to know their comely place. It is almost preferable— now that satire is dead— to see photographs of women holding assault rifles, an AK 47 or AR 15, angled across their chests. I thought of Rita Hayworth, her shoulders unabashedly bare, singing her *chick a chick boom* song in the film *Affair in Trinidad* and how far women have come—from the idolization of a sexually charged woman to the black bars across the bosoms of the next generation of American women. I remain silent through all this cultural and historical embarrassment though inwardly I sing my mantra, my prayer, my adoration: *Chick a chick boom, chick boom; Chick a chick boom, chick boom.*

ANALYTICS

𝔉 ew people read Clifford Odets anymore, but there is a rather astute exchange between two characters in his play *Paradise Lost* where one character says, "We do our best," and the other character replies, "Not good enough." It is easy to understand the retort because there are simple answers to some of our most complex problems— cutting the reliance on fossil fuels, for example, where solar and wind power and other natural energies can supplant them, but most often the elementary solutions are disavowed by the deniers, nay-sayers, and the committed clowns and buffoons who pretend to a sagacity impossible to possess by those who study, who read books, who examine the evidence. Yet, even the most unlearned could recognize the verity of the argument, the presumption of facts. The law that comes into play—as fixed as Newton's laws of motion—is that incontrovertible evidence whenever it meets the intransigence of ignorance will always lose. A willful ignorance trumps an elevated understanding every time, so, because I have lived awhile, although not necessarily always lived well, I am taking my physician's advice and ignoring the news, disavowing the world. No more anger and angst at the world's foolish proclivities. BTW, I've always hated clowns, circuses banal and crass, about as funny as clown feet. There is a term for people who believe they are smarter than they are, but even if this were encoded everywhere in our culture, those people, often in positions of lofty importance, would not comprehend the limits of their own ignorance, and they would flock together with those of similar incapabilities. So, I am offering my own world view, hardly the form of enlightenment gleaned under the Bo tree, but here it is. My own philosophy, expounded as I retreat, my own first noble truth! Don't ------- Oh to hell with this. There are birds at the feeder, winged around the bird bath awaiting their turn at the seed, and a ground squirrel is sliding down a metal pole leading to those feeders, the pole coated with vegetable oil. I've coated this pole with the slickest oil I can find, a greasy, pinguid, oleaginous deterrent, the folly of climbing this greased pole evident even to the ignorant, yet they try again and again, a slapstick comedy I appreciate because no counter argument obtains. They slide down magnificently in a wondrous ballet. Oh, the wonders of ratiocination. Problem solved.

AN APOLOGY TO MY STUDENTS

Always, when students ask me what a word means, I am struck by my inability to offer a meaning, satisfactory in its simplicity, its directness, knowing the question requires but a modest response, not an entire or thoroughly rigorous monograph, no OED history of a word's transmutations through time, its etymologies, its wedding of sound to sense. Asked to define simple words like "implacable" or "inscrutable" from Conrad's line in *Heart of Darkness*, "It was the stillness of an implacable force brooding over an inscrutable intention," I am lost, struck dumb. Those words within the context of the sentence possessed of meaning far beyond what a dictionary provides, and, without the sentence, meaning almost banal by contrast. Such the pallor of an eisegetical approach. I am speechless in my response, a doddering oaf of great pretense and little substance. Students may think me quite the comical buffoon, a man teaching the literature read many times, taught as many times or more, and still no command of the words the author employs, and thusly they may assume I know as little as they do, demonstrating the inutility of expanding one's literary vocabulary, of learning the language. But I am not capable of definition, of even the most cursory understanding of a word because that word is as open as the manifest meaning of the universe—every word a coded enigma, every word undefinable, every word a poem.

HARDLY

Hardly an uplifting morning. A child was shot because her basketball dribbled into a neighbor's yard, and a young woman was killed when teenagers threw rocks from an overpass onto traffic below, and, on a lighter note, a renowned biophysicist reminds the world in his new book promoted on TV, that 99 ½ % of all species evolved on this planet have perished. It seems our god is given to annihilation. Sometimes, on mornings like this, I am given to fits of cogitation: "So, the meaning of life is extinction, extirpation," I muse to myself laughing at the futility, finally solving the mystery. "What other lesson can one draw from billions of years of evolutionary history?" Once when young, as many youngsters do, I read Nietzsche. Took to heart the Higher Man, that freedom of spirit, believing individuality was a virtue to be uncorrupted by this mortal life. To what end? To what purpose? The salt sea disappears. The garden spoiled and toxic. But silly to dwell on this embryonic state. My old friend Melville—always pithily engaging— said it best: *There are certain queer times and occasions in this strange mixed affair we call life when a man takes this whole universe for a vast practical joke, though the wit thereof he but dimly discerns, and more than suspects that the joke is at nobody's expense but his own. However, nothing dispirits, and nothing seems worth while disputing.* Let my impact be noiseless. Let my mornings fill with hummingbirds at the feeder. Perhaps a few words written without disputation to remind me of this life, the finitude and luxury of it all.

A CONVERSATION

A colleague says, "Your wife is very nice, but she's hard to talk to." I say, "I didn't marry her because she is a brilliant conversationalist, a riveting raconteur. What is scintillating is not in our verbal repartee. If I want a brilliant conversation, I will talk to myself. I've learned a lot that way, have been much better informed because of it. And I have much to say." Later, recalling that silly criticism, I think to myself that there are times when it is better to be wordless, to listen to the still nights, the moth-like silence that takes the breath away, only a modest touch between us informing the world.

A FIERY WOMAN

Some women blaze with white coals and blue flame. On contact they burn one's very soul, and, as always, when pain informs the brain of injury, all senses light up and respond. The pleasure completely superintends the blistering burn. Women like this, beautiful in every regard, are called— using harsh and brutal language— "high-maintenance" by those who have few inner resources to conjure in response to what is surely the most exquisite sense of enlightenment. These men find humorous the graffito that scrawls, "No woman is so beautiful that somewhere there isn't a man tired of her shit." Women of such extraordinary presence drain one's psychic energy, sap one's physical strength, make one willingly spend entire paychecks on dinner, on weekend resorts, on kayak trips down the Youghiogheny. They prefer Porsche Carreras to Fords. Thus, one must perform like a thoroughbred 911 and possess a similar aura or be found dull-witted and abominably slow. Occasionally, they will want to turn off that wit, overloaded with synapses sparking. It is good to hear her say, "Enough is enough" after long hours in the bed of night. One feels good at the satiety.

One such delightful woman was mashing avocado, and so I told her the guaca moles burrowed deep to avoid such an ignominious end, kitchen talk as I placed one hand on her waist. I told her if she listened carefully, she could hear them scurrying in the walls, making nests under the carpet. "Stop it," she said. "I am not listening, not paying any attention. Go set the table, and this time make sure all the silverware is in the right place—and the water glass." I heard her stifle a laugh as I left the kitchen. When we went to the Jersey shore, she swam out further than made any sense, as if she knew the whole Atlantic wasn't strong enough to pull her down. When we skydived, I thought it didn't matter to her if the chute opened or not; it was the exhilaration of the fall, the feeling in the pit of the stomach of an unnatural act, that Imp of the Perverse Poe wrote about, pushing one to the edge because standing back was the same as not ever being born. The absolute quiet as she floated like dandelion seed in the absolute blue, taking in the entire world, her teeming brain sensing the wonder of that world— that was everything. When she landed, her face was flushed; a great smile reflected an epistemic joy she had captured far removed from her books. That was the same look, the same flush, on her face as we pulled our kayaks up on the banks of the Youch after an invigorating run in spring when the waters were high, when only a week earlier a couple of boys went over a small dam, got caught in the hydraulic and rolled over and over, tumbling, somersaulting until the river filled their lungs. It matters not how many angels can dance on the head of a pin if one has time in one's life with a woman like that. As she said making love, "There is more, much more, to all of this than is found in a life of the mind."

From readings in psychology, all those cognitive facts abstracted from laboratory rats, I learned peak experiences inform our identities, and such women, memorable in the experience, are what formed me out of some esemplastic matter, and yet there is that disintegration, like sphaghetttification as one is drawn past the event horizon and pulled apart atom by atom, once again just an array of elements and particles spewing forth.

Long, long ago, I had a Thai girlfriend, a Hmong, a Catholic. And God, she breathed fire. None of that submissive Asian woman stuff; that's all nonsense anyway. One of those women so demure and obsequious could carve out your heart and with some proper grilling serve it to her friends all the while extolling the virtues of the vegetables and the tenderness of the meat. Anyway, she was angry at something I must have said or done, and she wanted a contrite confession. I would, in a non-Catholic way, admit to anything if I thought I were guilty, and thus I am, necessarily, non-confrontational, seldom venting or harshly responding to the very ugly nature of things. It is a zero-sum game. "We should love one another," I said, "not argue about matters so trivial they will appear mindless and ridiculously pitiful in a matter of hours. Long term, the memory of this will be as paltry and as undetectable as a neutrino passing through a huge vat of heavy water." She was a stone wall when it came to my shortcomings. We went to a movie to quell her anger. She sat behind me and squeezed my neck, digging her fingernails into my throat. I had to button my shirts to the top for days after, a curious behavior in the Asian heat. Had we stayed together, if I survived subsequent stranglings, she would never have been satisfied. "I want all of it," she often said. Often. "All of it."

Yes, I know what you are thinking. Go to Thailand, find a woman who reflects cultural differences, East versus West, and then end up with a Catholic woman who speaks English better than I do, a woman who expresses disdain for Buddhist philosophy, its acceptance of things as they are, as they flow from one day to the next throughout the whole of a person's life. Bob as a cork on life's churning waters? Hardly a usable proposition for her. Better to dam the waters and turn the ensuing lake into a tableau, background for pleasure and excitement, a resort to nourish and sustain the physical pleasures of this world. Perhaps ironically, given the culture, given her supposedly obsequious sex, she lived heartily in the moment, and oh was she feisty. She disliked the time I spent reading, thought it a waste of the time we are given to relish the power of the world, the dynamic physical interaction we have with the raw and refined elements of existence. I was reading *The Cloister and The Hearth* with studious attention when she yanked the book out of my hand and threw it on the bed. "I am not going to sit here tonight watching you read a book. Edification is found in experience not a silly contemplation of things already considered. Even a momentary presence in the world is worth more than any sophistic novel." It's not that she was unaware of thought experiments or of reflection that resulted in some reordering of the physical world. She thought that reflection, pure thinking, was something done at an early stage of one's life, and then one went out and lived. There is a time to think about fucking and a time to fuck. So I buttoned the top button of my shirt, and we went out clubbing. Because she had previously sung in the clubs, she was asked on stage by the band and sang songs The Beatles wrote. I would have preferred The Rolling Stones though I could imagine her singing "I can't get no satisfaction" with a directness that would have demanded all my attention, all my ramming blood, in another hour or so.

Any evidence of human ignorance, let alone a willful stupidity, and she was vocal. She demanded right conduct. When the hotel manager changed my room—the staff just came in, informed me of the change, and started moving my things—she complained vociferously to the movers but more so to me. "Why are you moving? This is a disruption, an inconvenience. You didn't ask for this, you pay for this room, have been here on a lengthy stay. Stand up for yourself. Let them know you are displeased at the disruption. They need an adjoining room for a suite? Let them find it elsewhere on another floor. You are here. You are comfortable in this room. Express your displeasure, display some passionate irritation at your displacement." She pulled me close, grabbing my arm hard and whispered harshly in my ear, "We could be making love in this time they are tearing your room apart." Her whispers were loud enough to make the hotel staff smile.

I didn't care really. She would make love in either room, and she would argue no matter where I was staying. And her name? It is almost embarrassing to say it. She was not Lawan which means "beautiful" or Malee which means "flower" or Kinnika which means "beautiful flower." No, her name was Maria. And, unfortunately, she knew the song from West Side Story. She wanted me to sing it after we made love; I did, at first, but later with a bit of sarcasm in my operatic voice. Any of these Thai names were more appropriate than Maria. A flower she was, but a toxic one. Beautiful and rare yet one breath of that flower's exquisite perfume was lethal, and, as I came to suspect, not just metaphorically.

One night we made love, and an hour into our romp, she— while straddled on top— said, "I made love to someone else today." She must have known I'd be angry. She measured me, every response, made me want to have her even more. I was angry, and after we finished making love, I left, took a long walk along the klongs, through streets Westerners should not walk through at such a late hour, and angrily threw a watch she had given me, a Seiko World Time, all those lovely dials telling me of places and times I'd never been, threw it into the brackish, smelly water. It made a small plop, like a turtle slipping off the bank when startled.

To make up, she gave me silk ties, lovely Thai silk, ties I wear to this very day. Sometimes I pull one tight around my neck and imagine her fingers compressing my throat. You can't help but love a woman like that.

Another delightful woman, a Bryn Mawr girl before Bryn Mawr became a bastion of neo-feminist philosophy, loved to make love standing up, her back against a wall, her left leg held up with my hand. We were athletic then, alive in our bodies, every sense fulfilled. I kissed her knee as passionately as I kissed her lips. When we first met she was still on campus doing graduate work. We sat on a memorial bench dedicated to a Bryn Mawr grad who had gone to China to spread a Christian message. She was killed in the Boxer Rebellion. It was there, on that stone bench, that I first put my arm around her, pulled her close and savored the return of a kiss. I doubt any graduates now would go anywhere if money were not involved, altruism as dead as the memory of that woman's sacrificial zeal.

One weekend we went to a crab shack that had gotten good reviews for its all-you-could- eat crab dinners—not the Alaskan King Crab obviously, but those little mothers from Maryland, the Chesapeake Bay, the ones that are mostly shell, little meat, though what there is is delectable. Our table was piled high with carcasses, the spent shells of these creatures that made you work with a vigorous dissection to get at the pure white flesh. Her delight in the carnage, satiating her rapacious desire, was wondrous to watch. The world had to be cracked and split open to savor the wealth inside.

She ripped them apart all the while asking pointed questions about Melville's exposition of philosophical conundrums on perception. "Why did he equivocate on epistemological concerns? Isn't there some veridical truth or some codified, coherent body of understanding to be found in the very hunting of whales? Wasn't the quest a visionary epiphany, a doctrinal knowledge, in itself?" I answered each question as she cracked the claws and wrangled the whiteness out. I wondered if those crabs ever had an inkling that their existence was given to the nurturing, the sustaining, of one woman's desire to feel and know everything. Later that night, I picked a piece of crab shell from her hair. As I lay next to her, exhausted but fully awake, I smiled at Ishmael's understanding of himself, the nature of personal interinvolvements: "It is as much as I can do to take care of myself." But then, I would not find a small, sharp piece of crab shell cutting into my flesh as I turned over during the night.

On weekends, when we stayed in our apartment enjoying each other's rapacious wit, I would buy blue crabs and spend hours extracting delicate strands of angelically white meat, tiny, almost microscopic, pieces, an extraordinary amount of work for very little, and I would make her crab cakes. I could never make enough, and there was visibly a note of disappointment on her face when this meager feast was finished.

1,000 days is all that's warranted. Relationships are fragile, delicate as tiny threads of crab meat, and then—the inevitability. I can keep it going a thousand days and nights whereupon she has learned enough. "Enough is enough," she will say.

Once, after a break up, her letter hitting me like an anvil dropped on my chest, the woman I loved at the time came back months later to retrieve her wine glasses, her crystal salt and pepper shakers she had received as a wedding present for her first marriage, and some expensive towels and silk sheets with an infinite thread count. Soft rock was playing on the stereo. She asked, "Why don't you strip? The music is good for it, and your shirt is too tight, and the morning is warm." But it wasn't right. One works to that point, and to regain it requires all the same energy. Even more.

Attraction, gravity, is a weak force though it forms stars and planets; it pulls all that mass and energy together. Attracted to the flame one feels generative next to such a woman. The breath of her sleep, the French curve of her hip, sparks every neuron, making it impossible to descend into a deep and dreamy slumber. The presence of such beatific and wondrous love and flesh and power superintends everything.

And so sameness, some predictability, became a goal, an objective in future relationships. No fireworks. No fiery kisses. Instead a kiss like kissing one's grandmother as a small boy. Perfunctory, her lips pursed hard as canned ham. But the house was neat, money in the bank, everything bought on sale. The bills were paid and arguments were not on the grand level of questions, nothing on the eternal verities.

"Wallpaper or paint in the dining room?"

"If we paper the dining room we can't paper the parlor. It is too expensive, and we don't want to over-decorate."

Or, "There's not enough bite to the chili, not enough chili powder. It's really rather bland."

"Add more if you wish, but it may be hotter tomorrow when the flavors come through."

She might as well have said, "Be satisfied. I have rationed the chili powder responsibly, as I see fit."

Sometimes I sneak some dark, red chili powder from the Southwest into the pot. Most often she knows of my tampering. I can feel it, expecting some remonstration as any of my lovers in the past would have given, but she is mild and content, and she wouldn't know a Porsche Carrera from a tree stump.

There's a Ford utility vehicle parked in our driveway.

PERHAPS

Perhaps the only subject unavailable to poetry is teaching, recording the banality of a student's response in the classroom, the disdain for reading a text that has words and images outside their domain; for instance, teaching *Slaughterhouse Five*, explaining time-tripping in terms of Feynman diagrams, experiments with atomic clocks, the psychic defenses and dynamics of the mind, and *The Illusion of Time*, a masterful lecture by the physicist Brian Greene: the mathematics, the physics, work equally the same going backwards or forwards in time. And so, on the exams, they write, *It's not possible to go back in time*, or as one student said to another, *That's bullshit*, spoken under his breath, not knowing I can lip read a word as familiar as that. Why, even as I look into their faces I am seeing them as they were, the passage of light between us taking time, not as much as there is between a star I try to capture with my puny telescope on a cold, vaporous night, but still emblem and symbol of how nothing reaches to breach the space between us, as if us, student and teacher, husband and wife, old lovers from long ago, a book now forgotten, aren't receding—a retrograde movement in memory: the young rabbit I couldn't rescue, trapped in a drain pipe, washed out after a hard rain

TRANSCENDENTAL SCAPEGOAT:
A PARABLE OF ECONOMICS

Late summer and I am in a fine state—something of a snit my wife would say under her breath—anxious, wary, troubled by an imminent incursion into my garden domain. I blame Thoreau for my tomato anxiety, his lessons in husbandry, his instructions to plant additional rows of beans for the woodchucks who need to eat just as homo sapiens do in order to survive. It is spiritual sustenance, growing one's own food, and spiritual as well on another plane since all life is interwoven and interdependent, the Over-Soul glowing like a summer sun over all, blazing like tomatoes on the vine, and yet Thoreau, in laissez faire, authoritarian fashion, needed to derail his competition, like that proverbial machine in the garden he sometimes raged against, recognizing that enemy woodchucks—marauders and trespassers all—were appropriating more than their share, certainly more than Thoreau could spare. What was learned in the pencil factory was not lost in the bean field. Capitalism by definition means competition for resources, and it is the very essence of capitalism that everyone must fend for himself in this survivalist game of the fittest, thieving without getting caught, lechery under a Christian name. Root hog, or die. The time had not yet arrived for Transcendental Capitalism to capture our economic imaginations, nor would it as the Anthropocene tightened its grip. When Thoreau, puzzled by the quandary of mercy, mercy being an economic luxury, asked a fellow farmer how to control the thieving woodchucks, he was told, with a measure of derisive laughter, "Shoot 'em you damn fool." He did that once and ate it for his evening meal, the taste musky and unpleasant, and besides there was that violation of the rule to sanctify all life. So, from then on, no Bleeding Kansas in the bean fields, Thoreau trapped them humanely, as much Jainist as Franciscan, let them loose some distance away from his farm, issuing a stern warning never to return: upon one woodchuck's release he smacked it on its butt with a stick, a lesson such as that inflicted on a misbehaving student by a Catholic nun. I too have humane traps and could set them to catch the marauding thieves, but the thought of eating even a possum or raccoon let alone the smaller vermin (chipmunk stew, vole soup, seem especially repugnant) makes this dining unthinkable, unpalatable to my civilized American taste. And then there is the fact of killing: I am far removed from my grandparents' generation where they could buy a live chicken for Sunday dinner and snap its neck after church as if it were a twig to be thrown in the fire. I can still imagine the resounding snap of the chicken's scrawny neck. The taste of these fatted scofflaws tearing up my garden must be as repellent as that woodchuck was to Thoreau—a practical justification of live and let live philosophy, merciful understanding tempered by odoriferous toughness and an ugly taste in the mouth. Nor could this be shared since my wife would neither cook it nor eat it nor share it with even the hungriest of the homeless who would rather search through the neighborhood trash bins. It is impossible, as it is with beans, to plant enough tomatoes to satisfy everyone's appetite, and it angers me, a man not given to anger, that some miscreant has taken a single bite out of one, sampling it the way housewives sample a grape in the supermarket before deciding to buy, and this one now soiled tomato, almost ready for picking, a blazing red Brandywine, warmed by the August sun, now to be plucked and tossed in the compost heap where it will rot in the noonday heat. I fantasize with savage delight of the demise of these various thieves and vandals, wish upon them an angry owl in the night, a hawk with piercing eyes and razor blade talons, protracting and retracting those talons in the meaty flesh of its lunch. Before this season ends, I want one rich red tomato to lie sliced open in a radiating pattern on my evening plate, a testament to the world's bounty, my profound power to grow a beautiful fruit despite the pandemic, despite climate change, tomato blight, ground squirrels, gray squirrels, ground hogs, gophers, voles and whoever else slinks through the night, the predawn madness, to steal my garden's delight, the produce of an entire summer of husbandry. And yet, looking out from my back porch, this evening smells sweet and generous, fireflies and bats winging through the Prussian blue of the sky. I remember Uncle Toby releasing a fly trapped inside, opening a window sash saying, "There is room in the world for both thee and me." Overtures abound, and I feel biblical and Transcendental and even literary. I am large; I feed multitudes.

THE PROFESSION

Reader, remember the old photographs of scholars on the backs of dust jackets, a wall of books behind, the tweed, the pipe held in the hand, meditatively as if lost in a powerful thought, the subject of a next book. Now, all this is affectation; professors dress like plumbers called to unclog a sink. Old school, closet filled with professorial jackets, wool ties, shirts of muted, bountiful color, I know extinction when I see it. A curl of smoke lingers above my pipe, the paper half-filled with words that will not see the light of day. Mere musings perhaps, casual as a touch in the dark as the wife sleeps. Whatever words are left are better left unsaid, unwritten. Now a soup can's message is as valid as Melville's *Confidence Man*, unread of course by the young turks who have taken my place, part of a confidence game: so many takers, so much gambled and lost. Once, so very early in my career, at an English Department party, everyone to dress as a favorite literary character, I dressed in a light tan suit and a white, furry hat borrowed from my wife as bulwark against the cold Wisconsin winters; I exclaimed the word charity in every sentence whereupon no one got the reference, no one had a clue, and then a mild colleague who knew but one book having left the priestly education before taking his vows, asked of my character, and I replied, "Charity never fails." At least the inquiry when others shook their heads and walked away. "Believe in charity, my friend; it is all we have." Valuing his trust I volunteered, "This is but the first incarnation; the last to be Professor of English whereupon the earth shall descend into darkness." Facing his puzzled look, perhaps as if failing an examination, I said, "Take heart, 'there is sorrow in the world, but goodness too.' You simply will not find it here."

THE FLAT EARTH

A black spot on the X-ray, size of a penny, a nickel, the scale not known precisely, the blackness the immediate focus, the hard protuberance as if some crystal were growing out of her breast, and the blackness, the hardness, were inescapable barriers or obstacles on any voyage of discovery. How do we get over this, rearranging our lives that no longer are knowable, recognizable, that are lied to despite the one stipulation, her one elemental request: "I want to know. I want nothing kept from me regarding treatment or prognosis or the consequences or side effects of treatment." But they are trained to lie, to refuse admittance to that knowledge that may or may not break the spirit because the idea here is one of control, and refusing information, refusing the science as uncertain as it may be is the only mechanism of control that there is. She says, after another lie, another sleight of hand or mind, another dismissal of her request, of her quest for understanding, "They really don't want me to know, and they won't admit the lie, keeping it all for themselves in simple measurements, the ideal and the actual, the variance that implies sickness or health," and when she offers a rebuke to their lies, their dismissals, their arrogant assumptions that one can't really deal with the truth, the human spirit too weak, the science too strong, she is told, as if a small child told some magical story to account for childbirth or sexuality or gender differences, the greater lie; "You understand we are doing all of this for your own good. We are only trying to help you." It is a practiced statement, condescending, like the cop who has received a complaint about a stray cat wandering through the complainant's backyard, and because she has cats as everyone in the neighborhood knows, she is lectured as if a grade school student throwing snowballs on the playground, lectured by teacher and principal and then sent home with a note to her parents, and the cop won't listen when told it is not her cat because, regardless of proof, of verification, of some simple clue or a vestige of evidence, he continues his preachery, because he is a cop and what little knowledge he has is exceeded only by his authoritarian self-delusion. The nurses—like cops, or teachers, or principals, anyone in any hierarchical structure—are trained to do as they are told, and given the concomitant power requisite to their position, they worship their superiors, identify with them, those oncologists given to arrogance whose orders make the nurses' world orderly and blameless, and they can share in the cruelty with impunity. With some unwanted and thoroughly discouraged insistence she says to a cancer care nurse, "So, you are telling me that I will not be informed unless I ask and that for me to get the information I need, I have to figure out what it is I need to know before I can ask you, and then, maybe, you will tell me what I want to know." The nurse replies, "Yes, that's about right. We're interested in your treatment after all." After chemo and radiation and her skull as bare and shiny as a glass paperweight, she keeps the port in her chest just in case, in case it's needed again when a hard crystal reappears, when a black spot appears on the black and white picture of an x-ray, a reminder to ask questions, regardless of the answers, the lies, the misrepresentations and dismissals because the only quintessential questions asked ever since childhood are *Why?* and *How does this work the way that it does?* And there are no answers, only a defense of lying and lying and lying, a universal contract or pact where the value lies in acceptance, in patience, in quietude and silent appreciation because to ask questions, to request answers, is to weight the scales, to tilt the whole enterprise unfavorably, everything precipitously shifting and sliding and falling off the edge of the earth.

THE GUNPOWDER BIBLE

—Your country is desolate, your cities are burned with fire: your land, strangers devour it in your presence, and it is desolate, as overthrown by strangers. Isaiah 1:7

Reading further in Isaiah, I aspire to be willing and obedient, to put away the evil of my doings: I will become as a garden overflowing with water and flourish all the days of my life. But my heart, my old incorruptible friend, betrayer and betrayed, filled with a rage against untruth and injustice, burns with revenge—fantasy player, determiner and determinant of vengeful narrative, appreciator of eidetic, mind-plays that mirror eye-popping Hollywood screen plays, a lifetime of reciprocity that works as a minefield and concertina wire barrier to defend against all nonresistance to evil. Another cup of tea, a lingering tobacco pipe, and I'll calm down. But not yet. I want to take a heavy Bible in a plastic sack and swing it against the unholy temples of our race of hypocrites. No better use of scripture: except, long ago, having seized Philadelphia, the venerable British, marching on the Borough of Germantown, have no wadding for their weapons. Not like they carry rolls of toilet paper or worn copies of *The Crisis* papers or the *Penn Gazette* in their packs. So they stop to forage and quarter in that pious, pacifist, anti-slavery community, raid the publishing house of Christopher Sauer, the Pietistic printer, right then in the middle of republishing the first Bible in German for the people of the Borough, the Bible printed laboriously one sheet at a time in Fractur type. Redcoats, as blasphemous as they are impious, ransack the print shop, spill Sauer's Curious Pennsylvania Ink-Powder on the floor, remove reams of pages and cut that scripture to strips to be subsequently crammed down their musket barrels, ink-powder on their hands and boots, a lasting stain as of Patriot blood. No wonder the British are victorious: if you cannot win campaigns, despite the loss of your general, by firing the word of God at your enemies, though in a language they don't understand, something is assuredly wrong even in the heart of heaven.

MARRIAGE

My wife and I are watching a film noir series on the Movie Channel, *Cry Wolf* with Barbara Stanwyck and Errol Flynn. The film is interrupted by one of those horrific ASPCA pleas for donations, the plea featuring a number of malnourished and mistreated animals, numerous dogs and a few cats. The commercial shows someone giving a small dog a bowl of milk to drink. "I'm not sure dogs should be given milk," I say. My wife says, "I never fed any of my dogs milk that I recall." "And I believe cats shouldn't be given milk or cream either despite the popular conception," I reply. "I know this because I read that in a cat care book back when Lenore gave birth in my closet when I was a young man and needed more affection than I was getting. Lenore was a great cat. Wandered in out of the rain when pregnant, carrying the offspring of a tryst with a Siamese cat down the block. And I remember cats shouldn't be fed milk because of the old rhyme, *Tough titty said the kitty but your milk is pretty shitty*, an old grade school verse sung on the playground that for some ungodly reason has stayed with me for decades and decades while other things—Avogadro's number, Euler's number, the rate of expansion of the universe, the phone number of an old girlfriend, the date of our anniversary—have all escaped me." My wife sighs and turns over, burying her thoughts in a pillow. "I wonder how many verses of *Greasy, grimy, gopher guts* I can recite, I murmur, trying to keep the conversation alive.

EVERYTHING IN BLACK AND WHITE

On my way to work, I passed the new high school with the new black track circling the athletic field. Immaculate white lines separated the lanes, and the track glistened in the morning light like a new toy under the Christmas tree. But this was spring— time of renewal, regeneration, resurrection. Actually, there was something religious about it, apart from the athletic ritual, the sacrament; I recalled the presence of Pastor Evans at church softball games, the white of his collar, his stole on Sunday so white against the flowing black of his robe: always the white lines defined everything, no matter the sport, the religion, or whose life was on the line.

I went out for track in high school, ran the mile, and ran it badly. Stretching exercises in the afternoon sun created no desire to run, just a longing to stop everything, to look up at the unfolding green of the trees, feel soft wind course through the grass, a desire to just lie there, stretching languorously, thinking of slowing things down, of putting my arm around my girlfriend, Michelle, touching the slight dampness around her waist as we walked in the warm sun after school on a day I skipped practice.

Seeing the new track, I remembered the old, a cinder oval around the football field: my shoes were cracked with sweat from other runners in other seasons, and the spikes were dull as the mind of a high school history teacher. Only the best runners were issued the new shoes, and mine were hard, almost brittle, and the uncushioned shock of each stride ran up the bones of my leg like stray current from a leaking appliance. The sound of spikes crunching the cinders still hangs in late spring memory, hauled out like old family photographs or a yearbook from the attic.

They don't build attics anymore. Trusses fill up the space, and insulation, layers of insulation to make the house tight as a cigar box. My stepfather's track shoes were in the attic of the house I grew up in. Once he told me he thought one day he'd have a son who would wear them. I never did. They were black with white eyelets and laces. When my mother moved after his death, the shoes, along with his track trophies, must have been discarded like so much else that's not needed in the afterlife.

I wanted to play baseball; maybe that's what all this was about—my lack of interest, my inability to run even as fast as I ran the first mile in my cross country meets. In the fall—the air crisp as a thin sheet of ice on a puddle after first frost—it was easy to outrun whatever desire burned inside. But in the spring, something slowed, and what I really longed for was the feel of a bat in my hands, a ball folding into the well-worn pocket of my glove as I chased down a leisurely fly. But baseball wouldn't have worked either since I could catch any ball hit to right field, but I couldn't throw it back, not with any authority anyway, not after my injury on the mats.

In wrestling my junior year, in practice, I went against Fubar, his nickname even before he joined the Marines—Fubar who taught me everything, how to sneak a drink of brandy behind the school, how to hold a cigarette, how to lose big at poker, how to take down an opponent on the mats with a move so slick it took him to state three years in a row. Fubar whose biceps were so highly developed he couldn't touch the tops of his shoulders. He did an arm drag on me—I knew it was coming—and I tightened up and hit my shoulder on the mat, hard, and something snapped. My arm's been shot ever since. Just carrying my briefcase sometimes makes the joint inflamed—it hardens like a gourd, and I wish I had just rolled with the move, just gone with it and turned his energy against him. Still, that wasn't the last time I tightened up; I've done it a lot since then. Just watching the Cubs in a tight game ties me up in knots an Eagle Scout couldn't unravel. And those are just the easy ones.

The Cubs just lost another game to St. Louis; it was hard to watch, almost brutal at times. A friend of mine never watches sports on TV, and he lives now in Chicago. "A waste of time," he says, and it is. But he doesn't regret all the years he spent watching; we'd get together on weekends in graduate school and watch a number of football and baseball games, watched Muhammad Ali fight to regain his title after his religious battle with the government over having to serve in Viet Nam. "No Viet Cong ever called me nigger," he said, a line you can't say any more, and maybe no one would know what it means anyway. And why should they? The one thing you learn as you get older is how little sticks: my pine tar theory of history—a black smudge on your hands for an afternoon, and then it's gone.

One Sunday, watching the Pittsburgh Steelers, enduring interminable commercials, listening to the insipid remarks of sportscasters, watching washed up ex-coaches make silly circles and lines on an overlay of the previous play, we decided, after a couple of Guinesses, to solve all of our problems, simply, the way Rocky Bleir would have run through the entire backfield of the best the NVA could have put on the field. "Let's tape all the games," Rick said in a time before the VCR. "You could put all the games broadcast on a Sunday afternoon across the entire country in one program no longer than a Hallmark special if you cut out the crap." Apart from NFL licensing agreements that prohibited such things, we thought we could make millions taping all the games and dumping all the peripheral nonsense: the huddles, the after-action reports, the half-time clowns. Twelve minutes of action a game—each and every game could be seen in its entirety in one afternoon or evening. "And NASCAR," I said, "Take all those races, speed them up to 312 mph, and you'd save half your life; there'd be enough time left over for some real quality time with the kids. We'll market this to the sports junkie, the guy who hasn't enough time to play catch with his son, the son who'd otherwise be off drinking beer with his buddies and watching sports on TV."

That idea, of course, predated the technological advances of the DVR, the cable sports packages available for streaming that allowed the sports lover to fast forward through all the time-wasting nonsense, the time-outs, the commercials, the injuries, the endless interviews that were the same speech, the same clichés, pre-recorded in the minds of the athletes asked the same old questions of meaningless value in understanding the game. A good offense beats a good defense and vice versa.

Baseball is another matter—the pace is everything, the anticipation. I often wondered why I moved a certain way on a certain pitch—no one ever taught me what to look for, but that instinctual move to where the ball might be if the hitter made good contact, that was everything. And it wasn't just a guess. But otherwise, if I had a nickel for every guess in this life I had wrong, I'd be in some Ripley's Hall of Fame and wealthy to boot. Joe Adcock was the best guess hitter in baseball Henry Aaron once said. Maybe he picked up the rotation of the seams; maybe, like poker, it's in the eyes of the pitcher. My eyes aren't as good as they used to be—early fifties, and I don't need glasses, but maybe I should. I don't read as much as I used to: what will any writer tell me that I haven't been told before, and whatever gets written won't be said as well as it has been by the writers I grew up with. And the stories I remember—we told them over and over—and especially the one about how we almost won the intramural championship—that was baseball as it was meant to be played. In our high school—we had no school leagues—we played in gym class and after school for the gym class championship on the playground. The diamond, the outfield, were asphalt; a chain link fence surrounded the whole school block, and that fence defined the limits of our field. The asphalt had been there a long time, had turned to a washed out gray, patched in places, and the baselines were faded; the painted bases— a sickly white after all the years of neglect—were worn as well, blacktop showing through making it hard for the base runner to know when to pull up to avoid a tag. The blacktop, with its wavy undulations, moved like a desert mirage and made catching anything but a routine fly a game of chance.

A classmate died going back for a line drive—he fell back and hit his head on the asphalt. I was captain of the intramural team, and we were on top, had lost only once, but the kid just lay there stunned, we thought. He died on his way to the hospital.

His sister was Fubar's girlfriend, and when they went out on a date the night after her brother's death, he asked her, while making out as if nothing had happened, "Don't you feel anything for your brother?" Even Fubar, who had the sensitivity of a pet rock, who joined the Marines after I helped him pass a geometry course in the summer, Fubar who came back from Vietnam even more fucked up than before he went in, knew such a loss should mean something, anything, but she was cold to her brother's death. "I can't do anything about it," she said. Her passion in the back seat, so wanted and needed any other time, seemed out of place, unnerving even to Fubar who lived his life on the mats and in the back seat of his '55 Chevy, a girl undressed in his arms, a case of beer in the trunk. And when he told us this story, to wrestlers lucky just to get a movie date on the weekend, he remarked of her unconcern, and he had never said anything of his exploits, in the same way he never talked of the war, and it was this lesson we couldn't follow; thinking only of her warmth, the beauty of her undressed in the back seat, not knowing what awaited the rest of us, one way or another, this unconcern, this misplaced love.

I turned in his last geometry assignment in August; the next month he was at Parris Island, four months later overseas. He left with something running, fielding, hitting, pinning couldn't teach us—some things couldn't be explained, though Fubar tried. "She should have felt something," he said. "It was her brother—anything." Fubar, who never went to church a day in his life. Fubar, a guy who couldn't pass geometry or history or English.

We had to learn for ourselves, and it wasn't any axiom or postulate or theorem Euclid ever imagined. Maybe that thousand-yard stare began in the back seat of that Chevy that night. Who knows? Fubar dropped out of sight after the Marines; only a few stray stories were told that were lost as our own lives took over. In strange cities, on business, I look in the phone book for Fubar's name and address. It's never there. I miss the mats, the crack of the bat, even those stretching exercises in the middle of the football field on a day lovely and warm and promising. And I think I miss the cinders as much as I hate them. The new track is blacker, the lines whiter, after this early morning rain.

DETERMINISM

Mark went to the store, the nearest Piggly Wiggly, and bought some eggs and a generic whole grain cereal filled with dried fruit, raisins and nuts. When he returned home, he couldn't decide whether to have eggs or cereal. It was a day that could go either way. There were birds and a few squirrels in the backyard, and so, at that indeterminate time, Mark threw out the last stale pieces of bread from a loaf bought the week before and watched as the birds gathered and feasted on the bread until not even a crumb lay buried in the grass. He opened the box of cereal and tossed a handful to the squirrels that fought among themselves for the handout, and to those birds that scattered and returned and ate until another handful was thrown and then another, each sown handful eaten to the sound of grackles and crows pecking and singing. The box empty, he watched until they rose and flew into the trees, a few of them disappearing into the lengthening sky. *Eggs*, Mark said. *I guess I'll have eggs.*

DEFINITELY NOT THE BOW AND ARROW WARS

My bows, my arrows, stayed in her basement for decades, my mother's basement, along with skis and ski boots, air rifles and cartons of books, Scholastic Book Service books, a child's lifetime of reading. I had taken my fishing tackle and in exchange left a duffle bag of army uniforms, helmet, helmet liner, pistol belt, canteen, a bandage for a sucking chest wound and some heat tabs if ever I needed a fire. My mother was patient, weathering years of my debris, my childhood left behind, almost recoverable, almost my entire life stashed in a large area of her basement. My bow needs a new bowstring, my arrows need fletching. Every autumn the smell of fallen leaves, the slight chill in the air brings it back. I recall lovely fall days out hunting, the perfect intersection of living and loving the world. One afternoon, I took my papier-mâché lion made in 5th grade art class into the woods and shot it with my BB gun. It was somewhat disappointing that it only made small holes in the bloodless lion. But those days were perfect in the woods, whether I got a squirrel or not, most often not. I would miss them by a foot or two with my field tip arrows, but close enough to make them scamper into the brush or race up a tree for safety. A spare bowstring was stuffed in a gym bag filled with hunting gear and other artifacts from my childhood, and when I found it, I restrung the bow wary of the age of the string and pulled it back, remembering all the times I shot arrows into the air above a farmer's harvested field and watched them soar, believing everything would always reach that high.

COMBAT ENGINEERING AIT, FT. LEONARD WOOD, 1966

There's little to accept, consider, or believe in all this except it was our first time off base, the small town, Waynesville, a mélange of bars, tattoo parlors, places where townies wanted to pick a fight with an untested soldier, and that was easily discerned given our untailored uniforms that fit like shelter-halves and our hair cut scalp-level, scabs still there from the harsh cuts barbers raked across our naked heads, dead giveaways that we had, as yet, not much training in how to fight. It was late as we walked down the almost deserted streets, avoiding the townies, and the first *thunk* took us by surprise, then another *thunk*, and another, into our chests, our heads, until the streetlamps lit up with locusts, the street crawling, leaping with the barrage, our mouths tasting the bitter green, and no one believed the war would last so long.

CHARACTERS, STOCK AND FLAT

It is a cliché to suggest all rules must be learned before they can be broken, and that they must be broken unless we desire the same old aesthetic response, a shop-worn perspective designed to dull our senses, tire our minds, until we scream and revel in the physical joy of a jet ski tossed in the air, fiberglass panels and parts disintegrating, falling, and bobbing on the wake, the jet ski split almost in two by an impaired sailor driving a speedboat with twin 200 horse power Yamaha engines; by impaired, we might suggest a woman in a skimpy bathing suit sunning on a pier. Let's say the jet skier was a punk who took pleasure in winding it out on weekend mornings waking families enjoying the lake as an end of workweek respite, R & R for the soul. Regardless, one is taught to care about the characters we write about, as if they matter, as if what happens to them is of any consequence: even the antihero, most flawed, perhaps brilliant but intensely arrogant. His obnoxious behavior is repellent, but, like genetic resistance to poisons, we are now immune and accepting of the worst. "I don't see why we have to know this," someone in the workshop says; she wishes only to work in the fourth genre, creative nonfiction, a woman concerned only with her life and the lives of a few Facebook friends, all of whom she uses to her advantage, creating a daily record of their silly crimes. "I don't care about any of this," she says. *Exactly!* I reply, realizing at this moment that I am missing a major teaching point; if I were smarter or more religious, I might explain the mystical, spiritual mystery of caring and not caring being the same. But I explain instead, *It's just fiction; these are imaginary characters like your imaginary friends when you were five. They are just like us, men and women troubled by the troubles of our own making. We're like them, doppelgangers, identical DNA, untrustworthy, lying as we speak. Throw in a whiz-bang, flash/stun grenade and we'll all react with the same blindness, our ears deafened, our brains mushed to silence.* "But these are our lives," they all say, "and you're saying we shouldn't care." *Precisely*, I say, *Now you've finally got it.*

BULLET EATER

Called *bullet eaters* when anyone spoke of them, sometimes with derision, other times with respect, these were men who killed themselves after combat— after seeing everything, they saw nothing, and hence they fed themselves a bullet, cooked off a round into their sacred temples. But one soldier took it literally, as if he were the platoon's comedian or someone so dumb he couldn't understand metaphor, the concept of multivariate meanings or interpretations beyond him, putting no credence in anything not seen or heard or felt. And so, he ate bullets, took a pliers and extracted the copper jacketed bullet from the 5.56 mm round gleaming like fool's gold and then laid a number of them out in a line on his footlocker and asked for bets on how many he'd eat, and once he swallowed five at one sitting, money piled up, wadded in his plastic cigar case. But that was before. After, he understood symbolic logic, though he'd not done well in algebra, never solving correctly for X, although he X'd a bullet for his .45, thereby solving for why.

B's

I imagine it's biblical in origin: we're made in God's image, are given dominion over the earth and all its creatures, and one of us, in fact, is deemed the son of God. Still, when I get complaints from students who received a B, even a B+, I'm a bit surprised at the quarrel, and not much surprises me after all these years in the classroom; my god I've even had a young woman lean over my desk, braless, letting me admire her young, creamy breasts while discussing her paper just to insure she'd get an A. But everyone deserves an A, just for being there, for showing up, for sitting in the back of the classroom and not saying a word, no matter the discussion: sixteen weeks of silence. You'd think students were novitiates in a monastery and forbidden to speak. The only time they'd ever talk is to complain about a grade. *I worked hard. I put a lot of time in on that assignment,* they'd tell me, whining petulantly. I'd tell them Einstein spent years working on a Unified Field Theory, and it all came to nothing—all those years wasted, not even one good and valuable academic article to show for it. A friend often tells the story of the time he received a B. He went to the professor's office requesting an explanation for this umbrage. He knocked on the door, and the professor, after a long pause, said, *Come in.* The professor was typing, a thick manuscript laden beside his typewriter. *Yes?* he said lifting his hands from the keys. My friend explained, *My paper received a B; this is the first time I've ever been given a B.* The professor digested this fact for a moment and then replied, *Imagine that!* and went back to his typing. I wonder where we'll go from here, all of us perfect. President Eisenhower was apparently amazed that half the American people were considered below average, and now with everyone expecting an A just for breathing in and out and almost getting it right, we have no standard of valuation. God's plan is perfect, we're part of that plan, we're perfect. Some of my students would say, *He'd give the Sermon on the Mount a B,* and they might be right. *Suffer the little children?* I'd definitely suggest rewriting that line especially since it's the little children who have contributed to the intellectual decline of Western Civilization. A ruthless editing is required, always. By the way, her breasts were perfect, definitely deserving an A, and, in case you were wondering, I'm giving myself a B, a solid B, on this one.

APPRAISAL

Only once or twice as I was growing up did my mother point out to me the tree that killed my father. The night of the accident, his bowling team was driving back from a tournament celebrating their success. There are pictures of his team in a box of family photos, newspaper clippings of his perfect 300 games, photos of him in his coffin. He was a handsome man, even in death; my wife always said he looked like a movie star of the time. No Hollywood lifestyle, however, although he was a pilot and flew to the Dakotas to hunt game every fall. The steering mechanism on the new Ford broke, and the car swerved off the road—a straight patch and the weather was good—killed him and two of his friends. I lost my father and my mother her husband, but after a long drawn- out, well-publicized trial, she got enough in settlement from Ford for a down payment on a house. A solid exchange of values. Henry Ford, history records, believed in reincarnation, genius the result of many past lives well-lived, compensation or consolation of no immediate value whatsoever to my family. An attorney once told me, matter of factly, as if codified in the law, it is less costly if someone dies in an accident; the insurance company pays far less than for someone suffering injuries for the rest of his life. I like how we assign values, a capitalistic virtue. $88.20 a month for military service during Vietnam. A $10,000 life insurance policy if you die, $2 a month mandatorily deducted from a soldier's pay for the premiums, more than two percent of what he earned, but don't—as the clerks insist as you fill out the paperwork—don't assign your girlfriend as your beneficiary. Dear John, a negative value and apparently an inevitability. That's life. And the tree—scars on its trunk visible for years— I believe it's gone, cut down or bulldozed when the road was widened out by the airport. If my mother had driven by in the long years after, she was driving a Chrysler, the only make of automobile she ever owned or trusted. I imagine she looked up at the incoming planes.

ENCYCLOPÆDIA

At the city dump a man flings a box of Britannicas into the dumpster, bindings touched with a hint of gray— mold or mildew— as if they've been living in a basement. I say, "Are you sure you want to toss those? They don't print them anymore." He replies, "I've got no use for them any longer; the kids are about to graduate, and they only use the Internet—wouldn't think of cracking a book. I just don't need a whole set taking up space." He tosses another box. A heavy volume flies open as if to provide one last piece of information to the world, and then another as the wind flips to another page. "Something is lost when reading on a computer screen," I say. "Books and newspapers just don't seem to work as well online—or magazines." Our small talk ends with a cliché: he says, heaving his last box, "The world has changed; t'was ever thus." I swing a trash bag filled with useless junk pulled from the garage earlier in the day, swing it over the edge, listen to it clatter as it settles in. I slam the back end of the station wagon shut and drive away. He does the same. We pass the cemetery of old TV's awaiting disposal, heavy CRT's, blank screens like headstones worn by ages, blank as faces blissfully forgotten. The flat screens that replace them are lighter, bigger, smarter. I think of Darwin, the *Beagle's* voyage, how change is the basis of all life on earth. The certainty of extinction. Ammonites are found high in the Rockies. I wonder what will happen to my eleventh edition, the Scholar's Edition published in 1910. Back home, I take a volume down from the highest shelf, a shelf I haven't been to in years: the binding cracks slightly when opened. I turn to an entry randomly: the Round Towers of Ireland, and elsewhere an illustration of Zeiss's Dipping Refractometer. I pull another volume, admire the learning behind the article on Palaeography, and then unfold the map of the Pacific, yearning in a Melvillean way for the Phoenix Islands, the Ellice. I remember the joy of reading, those early years of exploration thumbing through various volumes, finding esoteric things that made the world wild and untamable with its promise. My wife calls from downstairs, says we need to get the leaves raked to the curb—leaf pickup is on Wednesday of the coming week. I daydream a moment longer, then jam the volume back in its proper place.

FICTION

Most assuredly, almost certainly, the world lies spread out before us like a compelling yet bewildering fiction. Truth and meaning laid bare or buried. We like that as a species—the openness, the possibility, the selective closing down, the moments that define us. There should be few, if any, characters in this panorama, merely observation, a celebration like communion, kneeling with acceptance. In each life a second coming. In the days of book salesmen: the *Grolier Encyclopedia*, *The Harvard Classics*, *Great Books of the Western World*, a salesman says, "I've always believed there is a book, a story, in everyone, and these books are never written." That is a point, a sharp point of observation, but the story is not the story itself but the telling, the living. An acute immediacy. Life is episodic, and the episodes do not always cohere. No integral plot intertwining the moments. These discrete moments or events are the sustainable images of one's life much like the frames of a film—they are separate but form a continuous whole: the cliché *a point in time* is just that, a clichéd observation that hints of little value. Time is otherwise. Duration, immediacy, simultaneity—subjected to introspection and memory—define the fiction. Now, physicists argue the very concept of time is an error in perception, time an illusion, a fiction in itself. Yet we argue for the continuous, life from beginning to end. A straight line the only distance between entry and exit points. The peak moments inform our internal clocks, personal or subjective time, as opposed to that time measured by material time pieces: the Seth Thomas clock on the mantle, the Seiko World Time watch on the wrist, the ubiquitous smart phone that flashes the digital time when awakened, such are purely mechanistic measures or appraisals of what passes. Our internal clocks move rapidly or slowly in accord with various psychic determinants, as should the stories we preserve, crafting the story, the imaginative recollection, as if in some other space-time continuum and then the return. The art of memory moves with narrative celerity, so fast much is easily lost. Having a story within is only half the battle. Fiction spins from the cognitive unconscious, that apparatus that mines the story before being tossed in the smelter of the imagination. Is this not like Buddha's *Fire Sermon*, everything in existence bathed in fire? But thinking like this precludes the story's creation. It is life after all, not its imitation, although mimesis may serve as bedrock foundation, nor is it a re-creation that is engendered there, in the mind, on the page, in the acute moments of realization. It is non-Euclidean geometry expressed in its most simple postulate: the shortest distance between birth and nihilation is not a straight line, nor can its vector be known with any appreciable certainty. Theory and practice. Show and tell. Necessary collocations to get there. The door-to-door book salesman, the clerk in a small, antiquated book store, keepers—laudatory keepers—of the flame. Quite long ago now, high school teachers spent their summers going from one student's home to another selling *The World Book Encyclopedia*: inchoative stories really, offered without judgmental interpretation. Correspondingly so, characters are often superfluous or nearly so relative to the crux of the experience recounted, the way myths superintend the stories that convey the myth. It is said there can be no story without characters, entities to advance the plot; nevertheless plot is an antique concept, a convention as easily done away with as the ritualistic practice of cannibalism. Perhaps, in this strange new world, the reading of a soup can label can pass for literary study, or the reading of an anti-masturbation pamphlet issued to soldiers of the American Civil War may be as necessary to knowing the American Renaissance as reading *Mosses on an Old Manse*, at least in the way the literary brain responds to the veridical nature of the world. Did Emerson's early onset Alzheimer's affect his Transcendental thinking, mixing and confusing memory and imagination? Hard to trust one's self when that self is disappearing: in the wildly bewildering realm of physics, a particle and its anti-particle are sometimes the same particle. The hold those stories have on the self is tenuous: annihilation inevitable. I thought this brilliantly in that lucid, quiet space the mind offers—that psychic landscape of mental experience, and then the poor writing of it, the page, a pale imitation of what was thought. Thought is pleasure, and its violation, its interruption, like pulling two mating animals apart at the height of ecstasy. Pluralism creates the excitement: numerous points of view, contradictory passions, all interact in complex patterns—no simplistic whole, no systematic axiology. The interpretation of experience, its recollection or retelling are not the same. In what measure is there a degree of sameness? Merely a veridical capture for the moment, for the archaeology of the mind. What measure is there of a man's stories as he lies spread out for all the grievers to mourn? Each story a resurrection of sorts yet the stone closing the burial vault is not slipped aside in any passing, stories interred as well. All past loves are lost, all the skirmishes and tribulations, all the literary records, personal libraries dispersed. The book salesman lays out his wares on the living room carpet. The wares are tempting. What life would one lead with such knowledge contained therein? Would this life be any different? Would lovers be more receptive? Would the coffin be that much heavier with the weight of all those unwritten stories?

VANILLA BEAN

Buried in the psyche is a vault containing all the loss of a lifetime, one loss laid to rest after the other, an accumulation of consequence—like spices in the cupboard used but once or twice and sparely, shelved until they lose their aromatic bite. The door to the vault always is opened and closed quickly, allowing little time for escape. But there are times a whole procession escapes, one mad dash, one release, after another, and the heart turns black and the lungs clench at the remembrance. "I loved you once," reverberates in smoky shadows. "I still love you," echoes, time stopped, thematics scattering like mice. Loss like an aromatic herb or spice? How trite the metaphor, how trivial the loss. Loss is the permanence that glues it all together and yet we mourn. A girlfriend accused a previous girlfriend of never using that lone vanilla bean buried deep in the cupboard, accused as if it were a major character defect, a lapsed morality. Possibly. This is open to interpretation. As I seem to remember the glass jar contained two, long, dark vanilla pods, and the girlfriend used one, splitting and scraping the pod, taking the extra beans and putting them in the sugar bowl. The vanilla taste stayed there long after she left. But the second pod, the one left behind, had become dry, the pod quite brittle and tasteless, in effect another loss, easier to contend with, perhaps, than other losses, but they are cumulative, like radiation exposure, one dose adding to another. And if you are wondering why I am dealing with the trivial loss of a vanilla bean, a good friend was killed recently, and I can't bear to think about her death, the grief too great, so this bean—desiccated and dry—is all the loss I can manage, all the loss I can survive.

For Karen Buckley

A MATHEMATICAL GEOGRAPHY

If there is a proper beginning for this perhaps it was math class, algebra or geometry, it doesn't matter, he was good at both. There was a mystery solved in the answer to any difficult problem. Sometimes he had forgotten a particular method, something studied months before, and its loss prevented the solution; in a moment of acute recovery, he recalled the necessary principle, like a memory from early childhood, and the answer was there on the page a moment later. There was precision in the satisfaction of wonder. Later, but six months in, he waited in Kuwait and on an evening when everything was squared away, he looked across the border into the sands of Iraq and knew in a visceral sense that this was it—something deterministic, expansive as all history, lay ahead, and he could feel it, the geometry of this world in all the axioms and postulates he knew, blood-born as the landscape curved with Euclidean regularity. There was reason in the looming punch to his gut, but he had always known something, someday, would be unsolvable: a swirl of sand rose like an apparition calling, then disappeared in the latent glow of the sun.

Three years and two tours later he enrolled in college algebra, took a course in solid geometry confident he'd recover what was left behind, like battlefield detritus, souvenirs and scrap to be dug up years later when the landscape shifted a compass point or two, circumference purely referential and definitely not fixed. Time to move on he had said. But the quizzes proved harder than before—not the first or second problem, but those that came after, his mind focused on splattered points of light, the flash of a door bashed in, the cries and the cowering, defiance in their powerless eyes. Even the relative silence of the classroom annoyed him and prevented any transference of the equation to any recognizable system of symbolic logic. Lost in X's and Y's, nothing made sense. What he knew one moment was lost in the next. At night his wife said he wasn't the same as before. He dozed off fitful, edgy, as if unprepared for his next exam. He felt pulled in multiple directions, unable, even helpless, to resist, drawn as if by wind or water flowing through a disquieting sphere towards a belief as powerful and true as some mathematical proof arising from some barely sentient terrain, a belief that somehow a system based on an orderly construct consistent with his experience—mathematics and his tours meshed and unified—would become visible in the insistent recalling of figures appearing and reappearing in the swirling sand; apparitions or not they were there like fractals or winding numbers or multiple infinities on a plane where all lines always intersect. In this non-Euclidean geography, this was a given, an axiom with all the truth and sanctity of an explosive charge, a souvenir chunk of C-4 he always fingered in his pocket when only the irrational made sense.

A PASSING REMINDER

Bird muck reappears on the sundial as if a perennial remonstrance. Remaining snow cover on these irreverent blotches melts and runs leaving a slushy, gray gunk that reveals a last berry eaten before the snows came. On this sunny day in winter, the gnomon sticks above the melting snow like a sail. Every year I say this is the year of my demise or my salvation, and when neither deigns to occur I merely ascribe the resolution to some error, some cosmic rule of procrastination and backlog. Letters unopened mound the kitchen table, all the messages unread, all the words unnecessary. A traveler's lexicon of few words is preferable. One steps into a river of words, steps into it twice and it is the same river. Clichés and trite expressions scour the pilings; I expect bridges— like words no longer in use— to fail any day now. Whole worlds fall apart and I go with them, swept away in the torrent, a wreckage of outmoded language, phonemes and morphemes like vestigial ideas. Moving from shadow line to shadow line, the sundial insists on recording these passages as if memory, as if remembrance, were not passage enough.

ALWAYS: A PARABLE

It isn't just a body draped over the balcony that does this: any minute of quiet contemplation does the same. This could have taken place anywhere, yet so much would be dismissed if the time, the geography, were actually made known. *Really,* they would say, *that's ancient history, no one gives a crap, and aren't there so many places, so many times, much more significant, so much more telling than this?* Yes, all that is true, and still the man squatting on his haunches is right, an ancient look in his eye as he looks back, sees perfidy blossom as perfectly as the morning sun. The same question, the same inquiry, lingers in shadows of some past remonstrance, vengeance defines the very soul of the place, its very architecture simmers with hate. He looks away, looks hard into the heart of the question, says, *No one has ever kept a promise in this place. No one ever will.* He spits in the dust, flicks ash from his knee; where he gazes none of our gods can tell.

DRONE STRIKE

This is the Anthropocene, yet all our Thoreauvian reflections, our nature poems and prose works, suggest a contrary, as do our PBS and Science Channel programs revealing wonders of the natural world, the primacy. A tremor, an oscillation of sunlight, a hungry raptor circling, frightens the quarry below: rabbit, ground squirrel, field mouse or vole, always wary, always something overhead. If it is righteous of the hawk, it is righteous of the Raptor. We are all waiting for the kill.

FIRST ASSIGNMENT

In Georgia, my first foray down South, different flora, different fauna from that in the upper Midwest: Spanish moss and kudzu, snake birds and moorhens. I came home after a day on the rifle range training hundreds of young men to kill— three rounds through a bull's eye the size of a quarter for qualification— and found a small lizard had entered my apartment through a broken screen, something of a southern surprise. He lived with me for weeks during that summer. I gave him water, even kept an inch or two in the bathtub, caught a few houseflies and placed them strategically where he kept his quarters. He seemed a bit shy so I did most of the talking, thankful for the company. But perhaps I had mistaken his shyness or melancholy for lethargy which could mean something was wrong, like a stray or feral cat that had been injured or had eaten some rancid meat to satisfy his hunger and would not come near if it were not injured or sick or in pain—some recognition perhaps that maybe some kindred spirit, some fellow living creature might be able to help. That green anole—I had learned its common name though I preferred his Christian name, William, a name quite suitable as we conversed. "William," I would say, "You won't believe what happened on the firing range today. A trainee, quite frightened as they all are of drill sergeant harassment, made a left face when he should have gone right and his M-14 was pointed right at the gold bar on the front of my helmet. We are lucky this evening to be having this conversation." A week later William slipped away during the night having made the wrong choice. That morning before work, I laid him down in the tall grass in the backyard close to the fence. I had nothing to give, nothing but acceptance, a few moments shared. Losing time, I got into my car and sped quickly down the dirt roads to the training range, a long fishtail of Georgia dust rising behind me.

PORNOGRAPHY

On camera, a secluded street and a woman walking, young of course, attractive against the cityscape, old architecture in an Eastern European city. Nondescript and unadorned concrete towers loom in the background. She stops, is asked to bare her breasts for money, a lot, worth several days' work for meager pay. She declines, is shown the money, more is offered. "Only that," she asks, "To reveal my breasts? Nothing more?" She is cajoled, assured, assuaged, until she softly responds, "Not here, too open." "But no one is around," she's told. "Okay," she says, unzipping her jacket. She unbuttons her blouse, lifts her bra to the camera zoomed in to the nipples. For more money she will have sex and thus the exploitation, the offense. But there is a smile the camera barely catches; this money will pay the rent for this month and the next. She looks up; the fleeting smile disappears, and the dull, wearied, pleasuring look returns, obligatory for the lens.

SOUL-STINGER

Never think the word *soul*; certainly, never say it in anger or disgust unless to conjure from some wild bestiary a soul-stinger, something scorpion-like—stinger long as a braided whip—that injects a just venom into a malignant soul and thus removes it from the pantheon of lost and tortuous miscreants, a merciful end even for the unjust. Not long ago, a court determined that sexual harassment in the military was just part of the job, to be expected in that culture. I want that soul-stinger to do its job, to exact justice. I imagine the thick, oily stab, the barbed removal, relish the fiery love I have for such a venomous creature.

THREE POINTS

Whenever I toss something into the office waste basket, perhaps crumpled junk mail or the rough draft of a missive, I am always surprised and happy if that surrogate ball goes in, no matter the distance. The same with half a lime crushed for a G & T after the work day is mostly over, tossed from across the kitchen into the trash container. And I am curiously ecstatic when a scrap piece of oak cut with my bandsaw ends up arcing into the scrap-wood bucket at the far end of my basement workshop. All this ecstasy because, as a young boy on my grade school basketball team, I threw up easy shots only to have them circle the rim and spin out, falling harmlessly into the hands of an opposing guard. In my best game in my best season, I scored three points. It is an interesting point of physics that when a scrunched-up piece of paper is tossed, some of the folds open and the trajectory changes—radically—as if aimed in an entirely different direction, airfoil dynamics altered, and the shot mimics my grade school proficiency. I know engineers study the aerodynamics of shape-shifting, computing the forces, but I wonder at the mathematical formulas used to describe the various permutations. What calculus would perceive the possibilities, the variant forces acting and reacting, vectors skewed hurtling through the atmosphere? I imagine the changes in course would be limitless, a number as great as the chance of filling in a perfect bracket a few days before March Madness begins to interrupt the lives of so many across the continent.

Once, in practice, I made a lovely shot from half-court—nothing but net—but the probability computations for determining the likelihood of me making that shot again would fill several whiteboards in a mathematics classroom. My paper airplanes can't find the wastebasket either, no matter how well folded and balanced. Chance and chaos theory preclude success. I step back of my desk, toss a balled-up sheet of paper—errant observations and musings in abundance—and watch it arc across the room. It splutters, un-scrunching in flight, hits the back edge of the wastepaper basket and bounces in with a satisfying sound. Three points.

I am as good as I ever was, actuarial tables be damned. Unruly chaos breeds beautiful, artistic patterns, and black swan measures govern outside the norm. Behind the key of my desk, I have scored three points. In a world where it is so often said that the only constant is change, somehow I have the same joy, the same delight, the same exultation, exuberance and exhilaration. Same as it ever was. I wore the number three on my jersey, still my favorite number, that number never to be retired.

BIODETECTION

Long years after the war, the war still with us, I met a colonel in the Royal Thai Army, a liaison officer at the Army War College as I had been a liaison officer stationed in Thailand those many years before—much to talk about, both of us engaged and disengaged from the great moments of our history. *Just another war in another century,* a writer wrote, dismissing our lives, the entropic change, but our conversation turned to teak, the harvesting of the great teak forests, how every stick had been turned into furniture for the world and the elephants no longer needed, let loose, found starved, neglected—like old soldiers waiting at VA hospitals for care, the waiting rooms filled, wheel chairs wheeled in, wheeled out—but the elephants—elephants taught to detect mines, their uncanny ability to identify by smell explosives in buried landmines, the border landscapes littered with lethality. Some brutal irony in that when irony has been buried like those landmines—sanctuary from poachers, sanctuary in a minefield, trained for another harvest.

SECRET RECIPE

Everything tastes like chicken. Rattlesnake tastes like chicken. Alligator tastes like chicken. Ostrich, giraffe, even KFC sometimes tastes like chicken. And so I imagine do the thighs of a golden woman at the fitness center. Dear God, I wish I were a cannibal— and a much better cook.

O good lord that is offensive even to me: sexist, chauvinistic, demeaning, entirely out of character—so why? The world changed while my back was turned, attention directed elsewhere: wondering why the radius of a quark is zero, Higgs particles penetrating my cerebral cortex. So my mind is changing consistent with the world, all those gangly neurons doing an about-face. The President talks of grabbing a woman's pussy; forty per cent of women vote for him. My brain is merely adjusting to the cultural transposition, a diametric shift in the ethos. I will eat chicken every night of the week.

DIY: CONCRETE FOR THE AGES

There is a long, long history to concrete, an ancient building material little changed over the millennia; thus its properties should be well known by now and by virtually everyone. In fact, Alan's roommate in college, a civil engineering major, expounded at various times on the miracle, the virtues, of concrete, how it hardened as it aged across the centuries, how it endured and outlasted wars and natural disasters. Whenever Alan saw fresh concrete being stamped with the company's name and the year of its pour he remembered watching a neighbor kid carve his initials in a slab of sidewalk after school, the concrete poured earlier in the day, and as Alan bent down to do the same, pushing his hand into the gray and jelling muck, a cement finisher chased them off and floated their initials and handprints away.

Years later, Alan broke up an unneeded walkway running along one side of his garage to gain more room for a flower bed. His sledge hammer made a dull thunk as it struck the walk breaking small clinkers with each strike. The chunks were easily disposed of during the evening hours by tossing them in the street torn up for resurfacing. A workman the next day looked puzzled as he viewed the alien rubble.

Another time Alan complained to the city because a section of the entrance to his drive had been replaced, an expense added to his tax bill, and the next year it was marked for replacement again because a corner had sunk down below acceptable limits.

His concrete saga continued with the delivery of two and a half yards early one morning before work—concrete for the backyard patio Alan had promised his wife. Three of his closest friends and drinking buddies had volunteered to help—but this is 7AM mind you, and nobody showed. "What do you want me to do with it?" the truck driver asked.

"They'll be here. Haven't let me down yet. Just put it on the pad."

Alan checked the time on his wrist and watched the large barrel spin slowly as the cement truck backed into position. The chute glinted in the early sun as it swung above the forms. Concrete slid down the chute making its characteristic, unmistakable sound, the sound of real work being done. Delivery complete, a large, wet mound almost monolithic in its sculptured presence waited for Alan's friends who still had not arrived. After the chute and rakes were washed with a hose, the truck departed as did Alan for the office, determined to level the pile after work; there would be plenty of time to screed and float and finish a material that takes days and ultimately centuries to fully harden.

Upon Alan's return that afternoon, he changed into work clothes, picked up a shovel from the garage and slammed it deep into the mound of cement: the shovel bounced back with a curse, and the hard, metallic **DING**, a cosmic resonance as of galaxies colliding, stars exploding, the Aeolian sound that serves as background noise to everything we do was heard down the block and into the next, shovel sparking off the hardened tomb, shock wave traveling up his arms, down the length of his body until it flowed across the lawn, the subdivision, the cosmos, like ripples from a boulder tossed into a duck pond.

Alan believed he had time, as everyone believes there is time: a lesson learned the hard way, but differently from that of his wife who woke up each morning for weeks afterwards and sat, coffee in hand, at the kitchen table looking out the patio doors on a modern sculpture— one day a stylized breast, another a termite mound she'd seen on a nature program, part of an environmental series on PBS. Yesterday it resembled fossilized dinosaur dung, *coprolite*, she said to herself remembering the word. But this morning it just rests there waiting for her imagination—like her marriage, her life, her place in the grand scheme of things—to solidify and finally take hold.

AFTER SHAKESPEARE'S *WHEN ICICLES HANG BY THE WALL*

Yes, there are certainly icicles hanging by the wall, down the clapboards, dripping from the eaves, downspouts, gutters and a last course of curling shingles. Thirty days. A month— but who's counting—of days below the freeze mark; it never stops. As for *a merry note*, whacking stalactites with a shovel does nothing but break the peace: sharp, cutting shards explode upon the walk though better there than on the heads of those with Shackleton bravery venturing out to pick up the morning paper, ice sheets coating the steps, swords of ice overhead—a dangerous place despite the serenity of winter, a serenity born of the storm's remains. Almost nothing moves in this frigid pallor of air. Even hatred freezes: would it were so in the headlines— another air strike, more collateral damaged. I swing hard at a thick, glacial flow of ice twisting the gutter overhead. It shatters, and the headlines break: just another day of cold and damming ice. And fire, always fire, somewhere, on the other side of this world.

CHINA GREEN

Whenever Louisa became nervous or upset, she would stiffen a bit, march to the kitchen and brew a pot of tea. If she were in a particularly unpleasant mood, irritated perhaps by Christopher's insistent prattling, she would pack tea into the infuser the way naval gunners packed charges into their five-inch cannons. The tea steeped just long enough for the tannin to taste less bitter than the memory of their last vacation.

"I want to go to Alaska this summer," he said. "You always fight this; every year you want to go someplace stupid and tame. No one goes to New Orleans in the summer. It's hot enough up *here* to fry eggs on the hood of a Jeep. Down there, even the rednecks stay in the bars until nightfall. I'm surprised they all aren't as fish belly white as a dead bass washed up on the shores of Lake Ponchartrain. It's so damn hot the pom-pom girls and baton twirlers find respite in those elevated cemeteries where they curl up under decayed curtains of Spanish moss and lie sprawled on the stone tombs of forgettable Confederate generals until school starts again in the fall."

Louisa sat in the old chair they'd hauled everywhere, a chair made in the forties with wide, flat arms, arms big enough to rest books, and tea, and a couple of cats on a day gray with fog and water droplets trailing down the window panes in a seemingly interminable midwestern spring rain, the rain itself working as an argument that won't end. She measured his absurdity the way an experienced cook measures ingredients of a familiar recipe.

"We went to the desert last summer," she said. "You wanted that shit-kicking wild west cowboy vibe that exists only on those TV reruns from the 50's that are played all day and all night down there. All those Westerners transplanted from elsewhere, believing they are individualistic, self-reliant gunfighters, disbelieving in government, and then they let their lives be ruled by petty regulations mandated by HOA's. New Mexico isn't exactly near Greenland, you know. There isn't a worse place to go no matter what time of year—all those brown recluses in the outhouse, the snakes just waiting for you to make one wrong step." She remembered their hike into a canyon on a triple digit day, the peculiar sound he'd made as a rattler uncoiled across his path, color of sand and stone as if the whole desert floor were moving.

"I've done that outdoorsy, wilderness, away-from-the-civilized-world thing with you several times, and I want to do something else. You can give in just this once."

Holding her cup of tea with both hands, she stared out the window. Two boys were playing keep-away with another boy's hat, a grade school antic practiced, in a way, Louisa thought, by some adults. The air in the room was heavy; unshakable words condensed like sweat.

They believed in the ritual; it had become central to their lives like once-a-year Christians going to church at Easter to renew their faith. They believed the argument was about something important, about who they were as a couple, as if being someplace else together would make them love each other all over again, as if settling things out in their vacation arguments would solidify their marriage. They believed in the common ground, the affirmation, the giving in, the making up in the late hours when the moon turned fog to light the color of tea. They could make love in that light: afterwards, she would dream of the French Quarter, the trolleys clean and colorful moving through neighborhoods of an Anne Rice novel. They would dine in fine restaurants that served elegant and exotic cuisine, the opposite of their midwestern fare, and they would bask in the extreme Southern, romantic deference of waiters, like something out of *Gone With The Wind*.

Asleep, as the moon burned down below sight of the window, Christopher walked across cold streams, fished for grayling and trout, and wandered the slopes of Denali with Louisa picking berries for breakfast at his side. They spooked elk in the early breath of evening.

In the morning, Louisa got up early, put the teakettle with its whistle removed on the stove and waited; the wiry tea—a slight gunpowder green—uncoiled like an angry overture of love before she even opened the tin.

CHIMERA: A BREACH OF MORAL LAW

The industrial warehouse was empty except for boxes and barrels of confetti, strips of paper, colored and plain, some newsprint and leftover Sunday supplements shredded by office interns. This confetti had been stored for years, and when boxes were opened the pieces of paper had sunk under their own weight, now taking up but half the size of the box. It was embarrassing, really, the waste of space, the warehouse unused, the boxes half empty, and embarrassing also because this confetti was to have been thrown for a conquering hero, a ticker tape parade long after ticker tape was a viable cliché. The hero had fallen, the flaw a minor but pivotal transgression, and the parade cancelled; flowers for the floats turned brown at the edges and limped to some lonely dinner table where a worker brought the best ones home to his wife. Years later—his transgression as common as a cold in winter—the fallen one somewhat redeemed himself, outliving much of the damage to his personal history, though no one came later heroic enough to merit a colorful snow of unwanted paper, and no one needed to pick up the trash.

A MERCILESS SENSE OF HUMOR

The penis is quirky and behaves with a degree of petulance as one ages. More than likely you are already thinking with some disdain that here's just another exposé of what is commonly known: the penis wilts with age like an unwatered petunia in a summer heatwave; it closely resembles a gummi worm in its efficacy and consistency. But no, I mention this because I am a die-hard Darwinian. Let me offer an explanation. After a small coffee or pot of tea in the morning I have to urinate with great frequency until long past noon. Then, and only then, can I run errands or do other chores away from home, but this is still problematic unless a restroom is nearby. If I touch anything cold, any object at all, that touch will trigger a urinary response. I am not talking about putting an ice cube in a drink or making a snowman in the backyard in the middle of winter. I am not a stage hand creating a foggy Victorian atmosphere with dry ice that creeps across the stage, ice that immediately freezes flesh with the merest touch: not so, I have to pee whenever I touch anything that is but a few degrees cooler than the ambient temperature of the room I am in. Any touch of water, regardless of its temperature, does the same, an imitation of the old college dorm trick of immersing a sleeping roommate's hand in a bowl of water after a night of drinking cheap beer. All of this is karmic, I imagine, for all the mistreatment over a lifetime that organ has been subjected to. A sense of decorum here, otherwise a digression of the sort found in an 18th century English novel would give descriptions of that mistreatment. I am not, however, given to immodest delineation: I am not Frank Harris nor was meant to be. But I feel some urgency to relate the insensible discussion concerning my enlarged prostate during my last physical exam. My doctor, a sensible woman given to practical solutions, prescribed Flomax to control the need to urinate during the night so that I could get a good night's sleep for once; otherwise I was awakened every few hours by a tsunami-like pressure wave catapulting me to the bathroom and then, of course, it was quite difficult to get back to sleep thus resulting in a day of brain fog, a fog similar in its obfuscation to the chemical fog employed by armies to obscure their movements on the battlefield. But Flomax, as effective as it is at controlling one's urinary urgency, has a couple of disconcerting side effects. One night, heeding the call, I stumbled to the bathroom, my sense of balance negatively impacted by the drug, stumbled as if wearing clown shoes, and I grabbed at anything I could touch: an antique dresser, a table for books and a TV, my wife's leg partially exposed from under the covers, thereby waking her with a start. I fell to the carpet, suffered rug burns on my knees. I rose limping, lurched to the door frame for support, all the while running my hands along the walls until I reached the sanctity of the toilet.

But the singularity. The orgasm. This time-travelling drug causes a powerful reversal of all that's held true for a lifetime. A reverse orgasm, "a retrograde ejaculation" as urologists call it, a strange reversal as if living in a Feynman diagram, but here the tide of ejaculate reverses course and rages back. "Retrograde ejaculation": and I thought such playful language was too comedic, too sophomoric, for the medical profession to embrace. "Retrograde" is largely a military term, a euphemism for "retreat." Well-trained troops taught ever to advance, to move forward and neutralize the enemy, would never deign to retreat hence the term "retrograde" to indicate the moving of men and materiel to the rear, to a tactically superior position. I have often thought physicians have little sense of humor, but the term "retrograde ejaculation" is fraught with humor, inherently comedic to the one experiencing this phenomenon. I explained my surprise at the effect, the comedy of it all, a confounding of the essential element that defines the male of the species. My humorous depiction of this phenomenon falls short, and my doctor is underwhelmed by my narrative, my profound consternation. "Do you know how many penis jokes I listen to in a day?" "No," I reply, "but abstracting from that you most certainly lead a more interesting life than I do." She is not amused, having dealt literally and figuratively and comically with the male organ throughout her professional career. I close off the conversation saying, "I am eminently curious and will take the drug one more time to experience the world going backward. Brian Greene has lectured that the laws of physics work the same going backwards and forwards, and this will give me the rare opportunity to experience time in a way neither Bergson nor the Romantic poets ever imagined."

I realize this is an age of dick pics and men masturbating in flowerpots, thus writing about the penis is problematic and alienating, certainly a taboo subject in many quarters, but questions remain even in serious literature: Mrs. Kendall, for example, who befriends Joseph Merrick in *The Elephant Man* is surprised, even incredulous, to find there is no bone in the penis. There should be; that's why high schoolers call an erection a "boner." From an evolutionary perspective this absence is curious: all other mammals have a baculum, a bone in the penis, but not homo sapiens. Curious and curiouser: I ask my dear doctor if she has not thought about why evolution has taken the turn that it has. After all, in medical school she must have studied vestigial organs, and she treats patients every day who suffer backaches because mankind has only been walking upright for a relatively few millennia, but she shows little interest—evolutionary biology not in the forefront of her medical practice. "No, that is not a concern for me," she says. I believe this lapse in her personal body of knowledge is deliberate, by design, as she examines me for a hernia.

Tonight, a last stumble, a last headache, a last loss of balance throwing me to the floor. Tomorrow, I will wake with a baculum-less boner if I am lucky, as

I have done for so many decades past, and in that fine state between waking and sleeping, a retrograde hypnagogic state let's say, I will repeat the collective evolutionary history of my species, travel back in time with this reversal of fortunes, a baculum firmly in place as I practice walking upright somewhere on a warm African savannah.

A LECTURE ON MISDEEDS

Late evening after a lecture on misdeeds, the vaporization of fellow citizens suspected of plotting against compatriots of a different faith, no due process, the lecturer, spokeswoman for the ACLU, needs a ride from the Air Force Academy to the airport. She has been dispassionate in her legal appraisal of Constitutional infringements. She visits rules of engagement violations with a legal understanding that is cold and distanced from the actuality of the battlefield. She is committed to a just and rational process, a legal determination. On this late evening drive, I tell her of the anger I wake up to: the daily news of artifice and dehumanization across the earth; what the culture, what the ethos, doesn't matter. I explain my lectures, both at my home institution and the Academy, how the concept of just war, just war theory as developed by Aquinas, Augustine, Luther, no longer offer enough for a nation that averages a military conflict for nearly every year of its existence. I tell her that, in my lifetime, our nation has radically changed: the old rules of decency and humanity no longer apply. Eisenhower marched his troops past prisoners in concentration camps to serve as a lesson, a reminder of reasons to fight that war. Now, even the bible, the code I adhered to in the Army, my counterinsurgency handbook, which prohibited the abuse of prisoners, has been rewritten, new rules for a new world order. Enhanced interrogation now permissible and heartily embraced. I explain that my students want vengeance, an eye for an eye, as they stay rigidly within the confines of the Old Testament. She exclaims the virtue, the preference, for an emotionally detached response, a simple laying out of facts in legal order, says she feels extremely sorry for me as if anger at injustice is a major character flaw, not an inescapable virtue in those of the world and not apart. I remind her of the venerable Buddhist rubric: withdraw and return, a necessary engagement and disengagement to maintain and contain one's semblance of honest pretense, a defense against the world. I tell her of a friend, a lieutenant colonel, who says he might succumb to temptation as so many in high places do: RHIP, and the abuse of power is an inevitable consequence of the very nature of authority, and who is to say that self-improvement is not justified in taking advantage regardless of the ethical lapse, and then what great accomplishments might obtain, the good that results, as expiations of bloodguilt, penance for the greater good: perhaps this the only way in our moment to purge the Augean soul. I think of the labor to kill the savage beast, the first labor, the beast within, a necessary anger at an inability to thwart or throw into disarray actions one disapproves of, violations of any modest morality: one needs the armor of apathy, the sword of *don't give a damn*. When one head is cut off, two more spring up in its place. I could tell her I wish an orange robe, a monk's serenity, the extirpation of the enemy within, but that involves a corpus of formidable deceit. If she were more receptive to my passionate entreaties, my anger at injustice, I might have shared the comical treatment I have received from the VA to assuage my anger. My VA psychologist has me curling my toes when I feel this anger swelling. Collateral damage in the morning news? Just clench my toes and then in sequence tighten all the muscle groups up the length of my body until the anger dissipates and disappears. I can't tell her I will take this anger to my grave. Instead, I say nothing and we travel in silence. I replay recent angers in my memory broadcasts, mind movies shown regularly like those on late night TV: shadowy figures out in the early morning hours moving through the trees in the hills of Afghanistan; an air strike blew them to pieces. They had to be the enemy or they would not have been out that early, had to be pursuing terrorist designs. But, they were merely women gathering firewood as they had done for eons, preparing to cook breakfast for their families. And all those wedding ceremonies: AK-47's fired up in the air in celebration. Those celebrations were met with death from above, the AK's interpreted as hostile fire on American aircraft. One might have thought that a country so devoted to family values would have been more careful and selective in its expenditure of lethal ordnance. I replayed drone strikes on a convoy of pickup trucks, the universal white Toyotas, stopped in the middle of a road in the middle of nowhere; the trucks were stopped and therefore up to no enemy good. An entire family killed, among others, yet the men had merely stopped to take a piss break. We paid them a pittance in compensation, less than a monthly cable and cell phone bill. "Sorry for your loss," the usual clichéd response. I interrupt my reverie and almost tell my passenger a lack of anger is the fatal flaw—nonresistance to evil a soft platitude, despite Tolstoy, and isn't it pretty to think so? I bite my lip sucking a tiny bit of blood and don't recite Malcolm's lines of demarcation, the credo I live by: *Be this the whetstone of your sword. Let grief / Convert to anger; blunt not the heart, enrage it.* But I have learned where such thoughts lead, such confrontation; we're both doing what we can. We travel on in silence, both of us filled with quiet vows, both of us driving resolutely through the moonless dusk, but squinting, or looking away to the edge of the road, when xenon headlamps pierce our solid thought.

A LITTLE LEARNING

The father says excitedly to his two children, "Come here. Quick. There's a Gila monster under the brush." The children, a boy and a girl, drop their attention and race over just as the monster slides off no longer to be seen. The children are only momentarily disappointed. I, however, am more than mildly chagrined. I had never seen one in the wild, but remember the monster fondly because my favorite fourth grade teacher, Mrs. Schomberg, had asked if I knew how to pronounce "Gila," expecting I would not know, Spanish not much in evidence where I lived and Gila monsters not native to Wisconsin, but I did, I pronounced it properly, knew it because my reading had taken me there, as reading should. I had stayed after school along with another student, a close friend, and we surrounded her desk for some additional teaching. She gave the two of us more after school than during the tedious school day, her curriculum constrained by the powers that be, a school board interested only in a marginalized education, emphasizing the three R's, as was the norm at the time. But after school we could go anywhere with our questions, anywhere our curiosity led. Sometimes, during the day, having mastered a rudimentary lesson, she had me sit in the back of the room near the set of encyclopedias, the *Americana*, while other students struggled with their assigned tasks.

Although venomous, the monsters are so sluggish you almost have to push your fist up to one's face in order to be bitten, and, of course, there are those who have done that on a bet or for the satisfaction of scientific research. The bite is not fatal, but the animal holds fascination nevertheless, holds us in its thrall as tightly as its vigorous bite, an almost mythical creature, venomous, a monster (in the truest sense), a creature magnified in sci-fi movies of the 50's to scare a gullible audience. I'm still gullible. I like a world wherein the bestiary has such creations. The monster is not fanciful, not a fantasy beast in an imaginary landscape. It is another ornament on the tree of life. And so I have worshipped this god of the desert for its expansion of the imagination and the truth of learning.

I received a number of A's in that classroom, the teacher rewarding my curiosity, my willingness to go further, dig deeper, encouraging and guiding my extensive reading, all those books that became my world. Later on in my education, things became more constrained, boxed and compartmentalized, one block of instruction, one discipline, never related to any other. Still, to this day, there are teachers, professors, who say history has nothing to do with literary study and the reverse, nor is literature to be used in any way to examine the society, the culture, that gave rise to such imaginative, creative work. Astrophysics and astronomy have nothing to do with religion or anthropology despite a proliferation of creation myths. War, military science, has nothing to do with ethical philosophy nor should it be considered in the light of various religious beliefs despite the large number of chaplains of all faiths serving in the military. Quite often, fundamental truths of science are unexplored when matters of faith intrude. Just so, I know so little I can't imagine the edge of the universe, space expanding faster than the speed of light, but I learned those A's, those fourth grade A's, were the only ones that mattered.

A GIFT

Always, at this time of year, citrus trees ripen in the Arizona sun and drop their fruit in expanding circles around the yards of fleeing snowbirds as well as those few, hardy warriors who brave the desert heat. Planetary in their configuration but so many and unwanted in these numbers, paper sacks or plastic bags are filled with this largesse: oranges, lemons, limes, that polyglot of combinations, and grapefruit, large and soft to the hand. These sacks, like bulging scrotums, are placed on benches dedicated to fallen golfers on these courses lined with ranch style homes, their yards decorated with plummeting fruit. I take a couple of grapefruit whenever offered though they interfere with the work of statins. *To hell with that* I say, willing to sacrifice my heart to the great god Lipitor, professing belief in the juice and pulp, a necessary verse in this scripture winding down. The taste is sour and by any seasoned taste, unpalatable despite the luscious, luminous glow of the fruit, but I eat them anyway, defying doctor's orders, resisting and resenting those perfect globes at the grocery store, my days dropping like grapefruit, a perfect communion, sacrament of the bitter beauty of being alive to this wincing pleasure.

CHARLIE, DON'T SURF

Body surfing off Cape May, the retired army colonel, the Marine sergeant, me, the lieutenant who declined the promotion to captain because I'd seen enough—I was beginning to break, I thought, and still thinking that as I swallowed a bit of Atlantic foam, the salt sharp as remembrance. My unit transported leaking chemical munitions, nerve agents, VX, GB, mustard gas, HD, by rail to Earle Naval Depot in New Jersey, twenty-eight days in a guard car, two consecutive trips: our rabbit died, our chemical weapons sensor, whether from exposure or boredom, we'll never know. The Navy loaded those containers onto rusted liberty ships, containers sealed with concrete and steel, designed to last fifty years after the ships were sunk a few miles from shore, before leaking again in the great Atlantic cesspool. The water cold, rest rooms too far away, we urinate, adding to the mix. More than half a century now, those containers are leaking, toxins knitted in the DNA of sole, flounder, blue fish—all the delicacies of the sea, the delicate molecules now coursing through our blood, as we body surf, measuring a drop-by-drop titration, evolution of the next mass extinction, the Anthropocene, our careless burial at sea.

SPARE CHANGE

Always there are the homeless, the poor, begging for a few coins on street corners in any major city, Chicago no exception; there's at least one disheveled person claiming extreme destitution posted at every traffic light. A good friend of many years completely ignores them, walks by as if they aren't even there. He ignores them for various reasons, not the least of which was his experience in the Army, forced leave after basic training, mandatory before AIT, and he had returned to San Francisco, walking home late one night through dangerous neighborhoods because he had not enough money for cab fare. He had been given only a partial payment of his $88.20/month pay because the government had trouble paying for the war in Vietnam and thus short-changed the soldiers conscripted to fight it. He had written to his mom asking for enough cash to travel back home for his twelve-day leave, and during the day walking his old neighborhood, his old haunts, hippies panhandled asking for money. He resented having to ask his mother for that $20 she kindly sent. And he resented being asked if he could spare some change by people who disliked the conscripted ones, a resentment he carried with him through the years like his old Army rucksack.

I most often give a few quarters if there is change in my pocket, a few dollars if I'm stopped at an intersection and someone holds a cardboard placard on which is a badly written explanation of that person's woes. I don't know why. I'm not that generous; I generally dislike my fellow man, generally dislike the state of the world. It seems a harmless enterprise, and my conscience is clear regardless. Another friend says, "All you need is a robe and a bowl," a platitude of no great import, and I'm ashamed it gets repeated in a myriad of forms. *Root hog, or die. Survival of the fittest.* I am generally unfit, and the gods are as merciless as the men they worship. I will burn a few dollars, inwardly chanting their names, and watch the curling ash rise into the heavens where maybe, just maybe, they will do some good.

SCIENCE, PURE AND APPLIED

She kept her vibrator in the appliance garage. The toaster, the Keurig, had to fend for themselves. I was looking for the loaf of bread that had to be in the kitchen somewhere, and when I discovered her vibrator, the cord wrapped meticulously around it, I knew she was the woman I would marry. I wanted to rush upstairs, jump in the shower where she was covered with a luxuriant, moisturizing beauty soap and kneel down, pleading for her betrothal. But I was curious; could she use that vibrator to enhance the whisking of scrambled eggs in the morning, to stir the gravy for Sunday dinner, to swizzle the dry martini she would offer on my return from work each evening? Yes, this was the age of the multiverse, multiple purposes and applications for everything. Somewhere, in the grand scheme of an ever-expanding, infinitely arrayed cosmos, I envision a woman in her kitchen, a rapturous orgasm as she smooths béchamel sauce to cream over her husband's bluefish dinner, her delight, his, a string theory dimension of quantum vibration, and that certain, proven, cosmological constant of desire.

REMEMBRANCE

It is like this flattened skeleton of a snake I found in Florida, run over on a well-traveled thoroughfare numerous times, its flesh gone, eaten by the elements, but the bone structure intact. I packed it carefully in my luggage inside several plastic laundry bags purloined from the hotel. I wanted to display it alongside a hornet's nest that had spent more than a month in the freezer, a robin's nest blown out of our maple tree in a late spring storm, a conch shell iridescent in the sun found on a wild beach years before. And there was this carefully reconstructed vole, bones retrieved from an owl pellet by my daughter for a science class project. The snake stank worse than asafoetida no matter how many days in the sun, in the backyard, on a half sheet of plywood sprayed every day with bleach water and soap. There are, in this life, some things that need to be returned to the earth, like memory, never again brought to the light of day, to sunlight and warmth.

PSYCH TEST

A favorite question asked on Army psych tests, tests used to determine your fitness to lead men, went like this: "Do you feel disgust watching a man clip his toenails?" I thought of this for a moment and recalled a writer who wrote, "Nothing human disgusts me," and answered accordingly. Such are the dangers of literature. Between blocks of military instruction back in the barracks for the break, I sat on the toilet, all toilets open and exposed, and our drill sergeant walked into the latrine, saw me sitting on the stool, and said, "You better snap off that turd, trainee. We got instruction in a few minutes." Ever obedient I snapped off that turd, not hard after an Army breakfast—bacon half-cooked, oatmeal clumped like coprolite. All the years after I say, "Nothing human disgusts me." The war in Iraq, the war in Afghanistan, the war in Syria, Yemen, El Salvador, Chile, the Balkans, Ukraine. Tibetan monasteries burned and the world watched making excuses. I crouched down behind a car parked in West Philly, police chasing a suspect. Apparently, he had run a stop sign, maybe his tail light was burned out. Bullets flew everywhere as in Vietnam. One of the cops rounded the corner of a church, the minister doing yard work, and he was shot and killed, God's work undone. There were no repercussions for the police. A friend told me of her neighbor down the hall, a young student at the university who allowed the police to enter her apartment, apparently looking through the building for someone they needed to find. The cops told the young woman to strip, searching for drugs I suppose. I was told they watched her stripped naked for a long while, told her she had nothing to worry about since they were both married. Nothing human disgusts me except today, and yesterday, and I imagine tomorrow where everything human disgusts me.

NUDIES

Now that there are so many more women bringing cars in for repair, my mechanic has taken his nudie calendars down, not that they were terribly risqué, more like *Playboy* in the fifties, but still, perhaps, not quite appreciated by female clientele. Things change; now upscale garages are as antiseptic as their walls, as if an operating theatre, bright lights overhead, technicians wearing white. This is an easy change to master. But *Playboy* without nudes, the *Sports Illustrated* swimsuit issue not a celebration of the ideal—if somewhat idealized—female form? Somewhat harsh, I think. And seldom, if never, a mention of weight gain or loss so no one is offended by her own self-image, the images of others. A while ago, the country pop singer Kelly Clarkson was criticized for weight gain—a pundit tweeted that Clarkson looked as though she'd eaten all her backup singers, and Adele, another idolized singer, was chastised for her weight loss; some fans felt "betrayed" by her loss of body fat, felt she should have been content with the way she was. Body fashions change—once dimpled knees were in—but William Blake's proverb, "The nakedness of women is the work of God" holds true, but I wouldn't put that quote, along with other pithy remarks, on the wall of a car repair shop unless, unless I wanted an argument or a contemptuous rejoinder. The male gaze and feminist philosophy forever at each other's throat.

Sexism, misogyny, are sometimes best dealt with using humor, always a good choice, I suppose, when examining the human condition. Thus, many years ago, when newly hired on the university teaching staff, I had to share an office with a female colleague: my space, her space. The office was stark, desk a gunboat gray, and the wall above my desk was bare. I put a poster with a poem on it to occupy that space. The first lines read, "Poetry ain't nothin'/but a stack of steamin' horseshit." Hard to improve on that, but the next few lines went like this:

> Give me a roan who runs like a
> Oklahoma thunderstorm,
> a bull that cain't be rode, and
> a woman who can, . . .

Dusty Rhodes (an obvious *nom de plume*, perhaps to avoid the spectacle of criticism that would ensue) was the author, but when my office mate, ardent feminist, lover of my nemesis Jane Austen, saw that poem, she said emphatically, "You have to take that down." "What," I said, "You object to the irreverence of that horseshit line?" And she said rather huffily, "No. You know what lines I mean." I feigned ignorance, pretended to a lack of refinement and sensibility.

I kept that poem above my desk for all the decades I was there because there are all too many who take poetry the wrong way. Truth and Beauty, Beauty and Truth, and the world has changed, just another evolutionary reversal. The freshman 10 has become the freshman 15, and no one is allowed to notice, at least not to satisfy the male gaze. The Andre Dubus short story, *The Fat Girl*, is no longer found in college anthologies, presumably because calling attention to a person's weight is a taboo not to be violated in our realm of snowflake sensitivity. Yet every year the printout of my latest physical records my BMI of 28, a nagging reminder that I am halfway on the chart to being obese and must lose twenty pounds or else—a perennial reminder hardly designed to make me feel euphoric.

The human male is no longer allowed even an appreciative glance although it has always been considered rude to stare, but sometimes I look at my wife the way my cat looks under the stove for a foraging mouse, and she catches me, looks at me strangely as I am thinking how beautiful she looks, her knees brown with garden dirt, now resting in a wicker chair on the back porch, a respite from the weeds, and I believe she is wondering, "Why is he looking at me like that, so intently?" but then she shrugs it off, turns her attention to the day lilies drooping and the hanging plants thirsting for a morning refresher from the hose.

I know things change. Political correctness. Thought police. The culture wars. Once, women said they wanted men with sensitivity, then they wanted Green Berets and Navy Seals. Once they abhorred the wars in Southeast Asia; then, when those wars were over, they wanted to join the Marines and enjoy the heightened pleasures of combat. I'm not complaining. I'm not entirely at a loss. I can process change. Gardening done for the day, my wife is getting out of the shower. She has put on a few pounds over the years, the decades we've been together. She's been a feminist her entire life, has kept up with the latest fashionable trends. If I tell her she's still beautiful, admiring the after-bath glow on her shoulders, will she take the compliment, thank me for saying so, think to herself, "Of course I still am," or will I get a swift kick in the balls? I think, given the odds, I'll chance it.

NOT A SHORT STORY

First of all, I can't tell stories— never could. Not even war stories though everyone I know who went to war, the people I'm closest to, all have stories, stories that captivate anyone who hears them, even those who hate anything to do with the military, anything to do with war. You can forget all that anthropological nonsense about storytelling being a universal human and social experience or how it satisfies some deep-seated biological need, some psychological and cultural imperative. Is it, after all, what makes us human? Man the storyteller, man the myth-maker? If we truly believed that, we wouldn't define ourselves as Man the Tool Maker, and even now, although we have discovered that a number of other species use tools, even some varieties of insects, we still think of ourselves as tool makers, men and their machines remaking the world. Myths are ancient history, literature an ancillary experience. Easy to see how tools transform the world, but stories? Think of all those people who admired Hemingway, not for his literary works, but for how he lived his life, stories very different and far removed from the real world. And wasn't one of the Medicis castigated for his interest in art, a foolish venture, when he should have concentrated on banking, the family business? Yet we still tell stories, whatever their worth, although, as I said, I can't. Every summer as a boy I went to scout camp, Phantom Lake, and at night, lights out, counselors gone off to drink or chase girls, we'd tell stories but only a few did it well, embellishing the plot, making characters come alive, usually tales of terror, yielding scary dreams, and once when a boy pissed in his bed, wetting his mattress, suffering the humiliation of having it propped up outside our tent in the sun, all day for everyone to see, we blamed it on the stories; they'd scare the piss out of anyone. But not me. My turn was filled with weak characters, uninteresting events, told poorly like a joke that's not funny because you screwed up its punchline, not like Bill Blackwood who could make up anything just like that and get everyone to hang on every word:

> The cavalry caught up with that Indian three days later, and they didn't bring him back. They cut him with their buffalo knives and carved tattoos into his flesh. After they made him scream, they broke the bones in his hands one at a time and cursed him and blamed him for every wrong done by any Indian to a white man. He was horse-whipped, and, when they tired of cutting strips out of his back, he was drawn and quartered—body parts scattered over the prairie as the horses ran wild slinging his arms, a leg, his bloody guts into the brush; at night the coyotes came out and howled a thankful chorus over their feast . . .

We were only eight or nine when Bill told us that story made up right there without any thinking, unlike the way kids like me stared at a blank page of lined notepaper and never knew what to say. Anyway, Bill and a couple of others kept us awake, alive, with those stories—even better than the ones told by counselors, over-rehearsed, time-worn by frequent retelling around the campfire. Last I heard, Bill had left college, gone to Canada to avoid the draft—probably a good story in itself.

I've gone over this story a thousand times, never getting it right. Once, I told it to a woman I was close to for a moment; she asked if she could write it; I said yes, because I surely couldn't, but I don't know if she did. It would have been her story then, not mine, and it wouldn't have been true. You can't live or write someone else's stories, and thusly so, many are lost because, like me, it's not easy to get them right. No wonder all those generals and captains of industry, Schwarzkopf and Iacocca, have ghostwriters to write their stories for them. Our former-President Donald Trump had someone write the mythical, magisterial account of his rise to fame and fortune, although that ghost writer later disavowed much of what was found there.

Even when we heard war stories from those who had been there, instructors at the Infantry School, those few candidates who had been to Vietnam before going to OCS, we thought of those stories purely in terms of old Hollywood war movies or those horror stories told in Boy Scout camp. They didn't register in any way other than the usual fabrications: Superman, the Lone Ranger, the Hardy Boys mysteries—all one and the same. My bunkmate, Dennis Goodson, had been there, and one night while shining our brass, putting a mirror-like spit shine on our boots, illegally coating them with Simonize floor wax, he told of an NVA soldier coming at him, high on drugs, yelling and firing his AK, spraying bullets all around his position. Dennis emptied more than half his magazine into that enemy soldier, saw the bullets enter his chest and still he kept coming, high on drugs, high on his own death. Goodson said to Rikkers and me, "It's dammed hard to kill a dead man."

Though true, that was an impossible possibility, convincing in the unbelievability, plausible in its undeniability—like the instructor who had one of his balls shot off. Yet, there he was in front of the class instructing us on infantry tactics, where to place an M-60 when attacking a train. If we weren't accepting, unthinking, twenty-year-olds, we would have asked, "How many trains are we going to attack in Vietnam?"

I was an instructor at Benning during the war. After I graduated from OCS, I was sent to the training center to run a grenade range. During my third week on the range, Malone 2, a trainee pulled the pin, got it arm's length away from his body in the natural motion to throw it into the pit, and the NCO standing next to him, an instructor there to pick up the grenade if the trainee panicked and dropped it at his feet, well, he was only inches away when it went off, and was killed instantly, but the trainee only lost his arm: a fluke; he should have been killed, but it saved him from Vietnam. We had to collect every other grenade from that lot and send all of them back to be destroyed by EOD personnel in case there were any more screwed up by a less than diligent member of the defense establishment. That was when we had full employment because of the war, and people were pulled off the streets to work in munitions plants: there were a lot of accidents, let me tell you. So, I had a couple of days off as investigators came down to make out their reports. Four of us lieutenants decided to fly up to Birmingham to have a night with some nurses. Rikkers had made contact with them before our turning blue celebration: blue was the color of the infantry, and our helmets were painted blue for the last stages of our training to distinguish us from the candidates who were still in the early weeks of the program. We all had to get a date and behave like civilized human beings before getting our commissions; we were supposed to be gentlemen, after all. It was a grand evening designed to teach us some of the military rituals, the social responsibilities of being an officer. Later, before attending the Colonel's mandatory teas, we would joke about the required socializing: *You **will** be there, and you **will** have a good time.*

Rikkers had somehow managed to get dates for several guys in our platoon. I had brought a date from back home, and when I introduced Jen to my TAC officer who was from the same state, Minnesota, he said, "It's good to see someone here from God's country!" And my date, who would not have made a good military wife, looked at him as if he were the greatest doofus she'd ever met and then instantly changed her expression, and in imitation of some of the Southern belles she'd been introduced to earlier, feigned such interest in him and our mutual state that I would have tossed all my cookies if I hadn't known it was such a good act. I learned this about her that night; she could act, and sometimes when I got on the receiving end of one of her performances, I felt lower than the most ignorant dud in basic training being hammered by a drill sergeant for once again fucking up.

"Why Lieutenant Trabert, I've heard you've made OCS a difficult and demanding challenge for the men in your platoon." Lt. Trabert was famous for putting officer candidates in the Chinese push up position, me included, for even the smallest infraction. Once I moved past him in a hallway when he was dressing down someone else, and I made the mistake of saying, "Excuse me, sir" as I walked by. He stopped me and upbraided me for the excuse me line, saying, "Don't do anything you have to be excused for. Apologies are unacceptable if your conduct is proper in the first place." I was in that Chinese position for ten minutes. Rikkers smirked, unknown to Trabert, as he walked by.

"Yes, ma'am, our platoon motto is *Lean and Mean* and my men are going to be prepared for duty in Vietnam. This is a perilous time to be an infantry officer, and although branch assignments have not been meted out as of yet, most of these men, your escort included, can expect to receive an assignment to Vietnam within six months of graduation. They will be ready, and I am hard, but fair, wouldn't you say Candidate Nevers?"

"Yes sir, you've done a commendable job of turning us into officers."

"Potential officers, candidate! You still have one more review before you join the ranks of the officer corps. Don't slough off now or you will be a private once again. It's always the little details that will kill you, Candidate Nevers."

"Yes, sir."

"Lieutenant, I'm sure you will do your best to get everyone, including Jim, through this program as a credit to yourself and your abilities as a leader. Isn't that what the patch, Follow Me, means to everyone at this school?"

"Yes, ma'am it does, and we must make sure only the best make it through."

"You are an inspiration, Lieutenant. But I see we are taking up far too much of your time. There are others who are waiting to engage you this evening."

"Yes, it was good to see someone from God's country once again. I'd forgotten how lovely and special women are from back home. They are really something else."

"Why thank you, Lieutenant," she replied as he walked away. "What a prick—no wonder we're losing the war."

"These rigid, straight-laced automatons who believe any mission is more important than the men are everywhere, my dear, and where did you learn to be that ingratiating?"

"Like the Lieutenant said, women from God's country are something else."

But we drifted apart; maybe she put herself closer to the antiwar camp, who knows, but I do know she would not have made a good officer's wife. I can't imagine how she would have responded to all those protocols designed for officers' wives. There were even whole books on the subject; I especially liked the rules for managing the wife's daily routine:

. . . there are four musts in the daily routine regardless of what you are doing with the rest of the day. They are:

1. *Bed making.*
2. *Dish washing, tidying up.*
3. *Meal planning and marketing.*
4. *Preparation of meals.*

Learn to enjoy doing a good job at your housework; have respect for your job and a mature pride in your home. . .

Depending upon your hours of rising and the time of breakfast, after which you see your hero off to work and get the children off to school, two hours should give you ample time to do your daily routine housework thoroughly. Of course, if you stop to finish a detective story or go back to bed for an extra nap, remember to deduct it from your leisure instead of skipping your household duties.

As for those infamous teas:

> *An afternoon tea is one of women's greatest pleasures and should be well planned with details given great thought. Do not attempt to give a tea unless you have a lovely cloth for the table and a tea service. This is one of the occasions when you should use your best linen, silver and china. . . .*
>
> *The tea tray should not have a cloth on it. The tea service is placed directly on the tray. There should be a pot of tea, one of boiling water (or better yet, a teapot on an alcohol burner) to dilute the tea if a guest prefers, heated milk, lemon with small fork or tooth pick, lump sugar and sugar tongs. The cups should be placed on their saucers, with the teaspoon to the right of the handle. It is better not to stack the cups, but have a waiter supply additional ones, as needed.*

The waiter?

There wasn't much there, however, on how to deal with your lieutenant/husband's death in a combat zone.

For some reason I had a hard time finding a girl in Columbus so I took up Rikkers on his offer. He'd learned to fly before joining the Army and had served in Vietnam as an EM before going to OCS. So he knew more than the rest of us, and he told us war stories, not to scare the shit out of us like some others, like Captain DeLoche who wanted you to sweat and think about it all of the time; he'd get on your ass if you didn't read those damned *Lessons Learned* pamphlets, and he quizzed you more on them than on range SOP. But Rikkers was soft-spoken and had a good sense of humor and thought there wasn't much you could do if your number was up, so he wanted to make the best of it before it was. One day he came out to my range and said, "Let's go up to Birmingham and have a good time with some nurses I know." No twenty-year-old Lieutenant can turn down an offer like that so, of course, I said yes.

Actually, now that I think of it, (I told you I can't tell stories) there was one man who wouldn't have said yes.

He was young, like me, but married and had just gotten orders for Vietnam; his wife was stunning: a body that caused every man to stare, a face that melted every resolve and woke up passions and desires that no one was even aware of; maybe she just short-circuited the cerebellum and made us operate with only that little node at the top of our spines, the brain stem, the reptilian complex, responsible for hierarchical social ranking, aggression, competition, and sex, the primary operatives in the military mind. So it was understandable why he didn't want to go to Vietnam. Leaving her behind would be worse than being captured by the VC and skinned alive. Not that the VC did those things, but Captain DeLoche said they did, and he had been there.

So, I understood why some men didn't want to go. At least this one, not with a woman like that. Rikkers asked John Stevens and Thomas Manley as well; Manley had been in my OCS class, although in the third platoon, not the fifth, and we'd had some beers in the Gold Bar Club, and we had hit it off, sort of. Manley had heard I liked literature; a lit major from Georgetown had told Manley I had an interest in art, literature, even poetry. And so, Manley walked up to me in the Club on a Saturday night and said, "I hear you like poetry," and I said, "Yeah, I like the compression of language, the sting of a great piece of literary art when it strikes you the right way," and he says, "I love Robert Service. Isn't his work great?" And, of course I couldn't recall the name. Why didn't he ask me about someone who's taught in college, like Donne, Wordsworth, or Eliot? So he recites *The Song of the Soldier Born*, a Service poem I'd never heard before and asks me if I know it, and I say no, so he recites Dangerous Dan McGrew, the whole thing, beginning to end:

> . . . *two guns blazed in the dark,*
> *And a woman screamed, and the lights went up, and two men lay stiff and stark.*
> *Pitched on his head, and pumped full of lead, was Dangerous Dan McGrew*

But anyway, he's disgusted that I know nothing of poetry and walks away, taking the beer he'd bought me, and I hadn't had a chance to drink even a slug or two out of the glass.

Later when we meet, we talk, and he jokes about my ignorance, but he's OK.

Years and years later, when I rediscovered Robert Service, even using his poems for various purposes in my introductory literature classes, I often wondered—given Manley's conservative, unbalanced understanding of poetry—whether he had ever memorized the Yukon Bard's *Ode to an Oosik*, a poem celebrating the virtues of the walrus's penis—not a poem to regale your latest girlfriend with on a first date, though a good one to share with mates on a wilderness canoe trip. Certainly, he would not violate the rules of early dating and would wait until more familiarity had been established, an awareness of each other's sense of humor regarding sexual matters. Despite the openness of sexual expression in the flower-power, free- love culture of the 60's, it would be unseemly to work that piece as a romantic overture, the poem, perhaps, violating even the basic precepts of a burgeoning feminist movement. Romantic ideals not always appreciated: not every woman, then as now, embraced an equalitarian philosophy of sexual freedom. Manley might have to save that one for some other time in our planet's fretful go around the galaxy.

Stevens worked for one of the training companies and brought his troops through on a regular basis. I'd been reassigned (I joked that it was a promotion) to one of the Basic Rifle Marksmanship ranges as punishment for my hearing loss, as if it were my fault the Army made me play with toys that go bang. This assignment kept the unit one step ahead of the annual inspection team. Stevens and I would bullshit in the range shack about all sorts of matters, military or not, and he was easy to get along with. He didn't waste too much time philosophizing over the targets the way some lieutenants did; he'd work with the men, but wasn't fanatical, and we usually got tight shot groups from the trainees with a minimum of hassle, and they did well on the qualification ranges, so we were both satisfied. He was infantry all the way and loved being outdoors; he hated paperwork and his CO always gave him shit because of it. Once his CO telephoned him while he was out on my range. We were in the middle of a bleacher lesson; I was teaching the proper sight alignment for the M-14 and also the trajectory of a bullet, the points of impact at various distances to the enemy target, the effect terrain has on the trajectory. Stevens' CO was livid because he hadn't cleared out his mailbox and therefore was not staying informed. The CO made him come in, read and initial each memo or piece of correspondence over the lunch break, after, of course, being chewed out royally.

"Not much left of my butt," he said on his return to the range. "And no one, not even the Commanding General of this fort can cut the grass on my behind. There's so little left back there, I've been skinned to the bone. I am no longer even a target for Charlie: send me to the Nam, and I will get me a shitload of medals. I'll need 'em to counterbalance what Captain Henke just chewed off."

So we all pitched in for gas and left at twilight in a small Cessna. The plane was white with green trim and noisy. I was beginning not to hear so well from all the ammunition we expended on the ranges, but I shared the anticipation, the talk of how these sexy nursing students couldn't help but fall for the four lieutenants with the biggest dicks in the army. I looked down at the lights below on this clear evening, looked down on lives totally unaffected by the war, everything moving normally as it always had, and we were just four guys out on a date.

By the time we got there, the sky was completely dark, and the earth was beginning to cool. We got a cab to the nurse's quarters, or dormitory, except it wasn't controlled like a dormitory; I don't recall all the details. But there were four girls in this large room with a kitchen and communal living room. The girls were cute, each in her own way. And they seemed ready for anything. After a week of studying, they needed some time to be young, to break loose from all the confines of the adult world with all its responsibilities. And so they talked little of the patients they had met, the chores they'd been assigned in much the same way as trainees in basic or AIT were given shit details by pompous, sadistic NCO's. We were just going to have a good time.

Sandra, the girl I ended up with, was lovely, and we hit it off; she enjoyed my puns, my attempts to impress her with my quick wit, my jokes to make her laugh. And I was good at it, even in that dorm apartment when all of us were trying to impress our dates. But I've forgotten one thing; there were five girls: Susan was a friend of Rachel's and Pam's, two of the other girls living together. Pam was attracted to Manley, Rachel to John, and Susan ended up with Rikkers. The other woman was Ellen. We talked, we joked, we impressed them with our bravado, our jobs, our army stories. We were athletic, intelligent by God; we'd read a lot, except for John who always said, "Why read the book when you can see the movie?" But nothing we did or said, and we were good, and sharp, had any effect on Ellen. We decided to go to a restaurant nearby for burgers and beer. And we pleaded with her to come along. "We'll make it worth your while—" "Right, all the beer you can drink, on us," interjected John. "I mean we'll take you away from your studies. When you come back, you'll be refreshed, in great shape, a short R&R, you'll get twice as much work done."

"No thanks, I have to study, really, but thank you for the invitation—any other time I'd love to. I'm sure you'll have a good time, and I could use one, but I need to get this reading done." Her voice was restrained, somber—no, not somber or elegiac or sad, but something approaching all that. As if there were something deep inside that made her voice sound as if she knew all the mysteries we couldn't learn in a lifetime.

She was my age, but older.

We piled into a big Ford one of the girls owned, eight of us, so, of course, some of the girls had to sit on our laps. It had been so long since I'd been this close to a woman. Sandra adjusted herself on my lap, and my hard-on could have been felt in Peru. And I was good—with less blood in my brain, I made jokes, told anecdotes, punned my way into Sandra's heart. In the restaurant, I said to her suggestively, "Perhaps we should have some soup. We could consommé our relationship."

Her laugh was in the middle range, and I thought if she laughed in bed, I would love her and spend eons loving and laughing with her, because what reason would there be to ever get out of bed with a woman like that? I had coffee after two beers and brightened up enough to make the whole table laugh. It's what I did on the range when I taught night tactics, or basic riflemarksmanship; I entertained the troops, telling jokes, mainly about drill sergeants who made their lives miserable, and the trainees loved it; it woke them up, and they did a better job. But God, I couldn't get those young trainees to be quiet at night; a herd of water buffalo would have made less noise stampeding through a rice paddy than those troops. How can you teach that? To be silent and move so quietly the enemy can never anticipate your movement. How many died, because I couldn't teach them to be quiet? To exercise restraint? To recognize the serious nature of it all?

On the ride back, Sandra snuggled down on my erection; it was there because of her, because we liked each other, and she knew I wanted her, because she was someone I worked hard to impress knowing I couldn't have anything that night, not with everyone else there too. She was incredibly alive; she knew she excited me, and she reveled in it, the mystery of attraction, how I wanted her, to share that mystery, because this was still early in the war before free love, before the relinquishing of commitment, and surrender spoke commitment driving deep into her soul, one, two, three, shudders like three quick rounds recoiling into the shoulder, a shot group so tight it looks like one round pierced the black heart of the target.

But it was Ellen I was drawn to. Her voice, what lay beneath it. "Did Ellen really have that much work to do?"

"She has work; we all have work, and there is never enough time to do it all."

"So why did you come along? Why didn't you stay home and study?"

"OK, you're all big boys now so I guess you can take a little rejection. You're all lieutenants in the Army. Ellen was married to a lieutenant. He was killed four months ago in Vietnam."

"Jesus, why didn't you say so before?"

"It was hardly relevant or conducive to a good night on the town. All of us felt Ellen's loss; we've lived with it, and you guys remind her of it. She doesn't need that, nor do you. You're invincible, like her husband: death is what happens to some other guy."

And then we dropped it. We joked, and Manley put his arm around Pamela's waist and pulled her to him in a playful way, saying he wanted her, all of her and wouldn't let her go back to the dorm until she was his. We got their addresses and phone numbers, promised we'd call and fly up again. They were wonderful and exciting and played along with our schoolyard antics; we knew we'd impressed them, that they liked us, that we were a good respite from the books. We were gentlemen, but we wanted them. Life being what it is we needed that promise that affirmed life from them, before we were maimed or killed, which was unthinkable then as it is now when I tell of this. I didn't call Sandra right away or write to her, but I thought of her a lot—on the range, late at night, every morning as I woke up with all that youthful energy and joy. Thinking of her made me feel good and alive.

We did fly up there several other times before we got orders, Rikkers first, then Manley, then me. I went to visit Sandra, but I really wanted to see Ellen; her voice resonated with a sophisticated complexity; maybe it was that literary training in college, but the tone of her voice, loss as compelling as the tone of some poem I'd forgotten that had captured a resonant inescapable feeling, unalterable in its fate, inexorable as hooking a trip wire: although the poem was lost, the feeling never left, like the image of Ellen sitting in a chair with a book, looking at each of us, seeing various reflections of the heart. She was untouchable, unapproachable, but her concern—an unperceptive initiate might have said *pity*—was there for all of us. Maybe Stevens and Manley never noticed, like I said, we were arrogant and invincible. I never let that melancholy affect my date with Sandra; I never let on to any of this.

Once, when Sandra had been delayed by an assignment she had been given at the last minute, I talked to Ellen for a long while; neither of us was any good at small talk, and so there were moments of silence where each of us was trying to find something to say, but we could read the silence and learn of each other in a way that filling those moments with words would not have yielded anything. I picked up a framed photograph of Ellen tossing leaves in the air as a small child; her mother stood behind her, a pleased and pleasant look on her face, and on Ellen's face, the gleeful joy of being a child, glorying in all the new found treasures of the world. I wanted to say something about her husband, but couldn't, and so I said something about the book she was reading, the collected poems of Yeats, and turned to *On Being Asked For A War Poem*. I said of course a good poet could write on this theme as well as any other; she started to say something, maybe she thought better of it, but she stopped. It was as if she wanted to say something of what she had gone through, maybe not, but she pulled back. We changed the subject, talked of a course she was taking, and then Sandra appeared ready for our date.

I don't know what the girls talked about after our dates, what they must have said about us to Ellen; but I doubt if Ellen ever warned them; I can't imagine her saying *Be careful* to Sandra or Susan and then explaining what she meant. In the same way, she couldn't say to us *Be careful*: as if we'd even have listened, as if we ever heard anything then. Yet, I was caught up in the passion, and I thought about Sandra a lot; she made me feel that I still had whatever it takes to be alive, to make others, especially a woman feel that same life-affirming way. We need that more than we need anything. I would have loved her; I could have better than anyone else. It would have been what I wanted. But Ellen, death in the pit of her stomach, was it there in her voice? She had changed. Perhaps it was some profound melancholy born of a philosophy of human mortality, but I'd only be guessing and trivializing and missing most of the important parts in all this. Ellen would have been like Sandra before; her husband would have been like us: invincible, arrogant, confident, professional, taunting whatever lay waiting in ambush. So, this isn't a story after all; a writer once told me there has to be a change in the character for there to be a story. No change, no story. Certainly, there was no change in me or Rikkers or any of the others. And there was no change in Ellen; whatever change there was occurred months before, before what I've written took place. Like I said, *No change, no story.* Still, I wonder about this, whether—in the science of narratology—enough coheres, whether there is enough human drama, certainly no corpses strewn across the stage, no Titus Andronicus hosting a celebration dinner, his enemies feasting magnificently on the flesh of their own children: nothing as melodramatic as that. I showed this once long ago to a friend, the editor of a small, unimportant journal that folded almost as soon as it began, and he dismissed it, said nothing was happening, no development, no plot.

I've thought about this over the years, written it different ways—you can still feel the twenty-year old speaking and thinking in places, but it won't settle out.

Maybe that's the way it is with stories, the personal ones, the ones that stay with you, that burn inside and never get told, possessed of some reclusive need jellied in the cells. How many die that way, untold, but defining the person possessed of them, by them, cursed and loved as much or more than a child. Maybe that's why so many war stories never get told, why so many of the most hardened vets are silent, unwilling to let anyone know. And maybe that's the beauty of it. Ellen: I trust she had a good life, that someone helped carry her through.

As for me, how do I explain in what is less than a story, that people are sacrificed for nothing, next to nothing, perhaps for a cause, some ideal, some excuse that is lost a decade after that loss by those who swore they'd never forget? How do I explain those who slipped by, who wrangled their way out, getting all the goodies, sucking off the Great American teat for their entire lives, platitudes spewing forth like lava, the vinegar and baking soda spurt and flow from a third grader's volcano. And that's the level lived on. Some other character should have said this, I know, but then I'd be a teller of stories, not just a faint and paltry mimicker of the Tolstoys, the Melvilles, and the Bill Blackwoods of this world.

On the flight home, the glow of the gauges made me warm, thoughts of Sandra, knowing I could have her, that I'd won; not even consummation could be this sweet. But as I looked down, a litany of lights for me to read below, I dreamed of Ellen. Ellen who could have taught me what I found undefinable, unfathomable, what I would later have to learn all on my own.

NO INCIPIT

It is like the historical saving of precious nails: a farmer, moving on after his land was depleted or because he wouldn't be left alone by those who sought his improvement, burned his house to the ground, and afterwards he and his family combed through the ashes, a few embers still glowing, a bit of smoke rising from timbers and beams, looking for glints of metal and pulling out the still warm cut nails that could be used again in a new place where the land was fertile and no one bothered him with vain scripture and idle talk. Hard to imagine that a kit of nails was worth more than the house, but there it is; values change like tulips, derivatives, luxury cars now bought for a song as styles have changed. And the same with ideas, how those illumined ideals of the Enlightenment gave way to expedient compromise and disavowal, a flux of dissonant reformation. I collect antique lamps because the light is so much more luminous, warm and inviting, a yellow glow under the silk shade, unlike that harsh new xenon white, a blue mortuary cast now favored though ill-mannered and rude: light, what centers the world, exchanged and to what end? I stop at a rummage, a lamp from the forties planted on the front lawn. When it's rewired, I will have the warmth of its light, what will stay with me as evening shadows crawl across the room, a light like an old book read and reread many times over the years, an illumination I can take with me anywhere I choose to go.

LIVING IN THE APARTMENT
ABOVE THE LIQUOR STORE

You are expecting, based on the title I've assigned to this, that I will start with the shots heard on a Saturday night, the petulant wail of police sirens, lights bouncing off my bedroom walls as cruisers cordoned off the entire block. But that unfolding was ultimately uneventful, normative in a way; the ambulance didn't even bother to speed away: the sooner a delivery is made to the nearest civic-supported emergency room the sooner another call must be attended to. I was thinking instead of a woman who walked the neighborhood muttering to herself, a rhapsody of inarticulate sound, a terrible blasphemy of human speech. I thought of her anguished cry that night when someone took her favorite resting place, a recessed niche, the inviting entrance to a department store. Her cry pierced the dark like a night heron's screech or a feral cat caught in the feathery dark wings of an owl and pinned to the ground, its scream piercing the heart of the just and unjust alike. The woman's cry stayed in the air, hanging over the street like an oppressive heat mass in summer. Even the man who was shot merely let out a low resonant groan and then decently left us to the usual sounds of the city.

HIGH IMPACT/LOW PROBABILITY

Something of a Renaissance man, Jonathan Smart lives in a landmark, an apartment building built before the Great War, a place once distinguished and desirable but now mildly run down, fit for those of little money and a modicum of taste. The tenants are reserved, neighborly only in the sense that proximity defines neighbor, and appear as furnishings in this tableau. Jonathan lives at the end of the hall, past the elderly sisters who argue all the time, though their voices are muffled by thick plaster walls. He is given to bursts of thought, imponderables a specialty, and defines himself as a creature of the 19th century, a man given to Emersonian or Thoreauvian contemplations, unsullied by the intrusions of technology, machinery often an interrupter of his thoughts, and just so he avoids cell phones in all their various configurations, still just barely tolerating the old land lines that are going the way of all media, switching from analog to digital, streaming the way of all flesh. Vaguely aware of gentrification, neither he nor his neighbors can envision renovations that will rip out miles of phone lines and hundreds of phone jacks installed over the years. He would not have guessed that the phone ringing while he is in the shower represents a call of some importance. It's not that he doesn't hear the phone: AT&T had long ago established a ring tone that is hard to ignore, hard not to hear with its raucous, ugly, unmusical blare designed to insistently irritate and annoy. But there is a choice to be made here: either step out of the shower and race wetly to the phone, only to find a telemarketer on the other end of the line, possibly a solicitor for some noble cause which Jonathan cannot indulge at the moment, or he can stay in the warm water basking and believing any important call would be connected later when he isn't wet and dreamy and non-responsive to the world. This is the error of the world, however. A matter seemingly of no consequence could entail a change such that Jonathan would forever after be grateful, a life-change that gives him everything. When the phone does not ring again that day, Jonathan notes he is better off. Contemplating what could have been, what was and will be, he rests in the comfort of knowing the nothing that is and the nothing that is not. *It is always the right time* he says, *always*, and turns the ringer switch on the phone to off.

THE WONDERS OF TEACHING AMERICAN HISTORY
AND LITERATURE

Always I was told by masters of pedagogy that there were no stupid questions, always told to recite that mindless line, "There *are* no stupid questions," as if it were a sacred mantra to be sermonized in every class in every course, putting all the stupid students at ease, and already I feel the repulsion, the anger and animosity directed because I wrote such a terrible, indefensible, uncaring thought, but who's to blame? Lies and more lies layered like limestone, the lies embedded deep in our cultural ignorance. So, yes, there are stupid questions, and everyone has a few buried under the skin just itching to be scratched into the world, and yes, there are still a few who will say said questions are imminently stupid, because dumbstruck stupid is the aim of it all, and still the classrooms fill.

GOOD CONDUCT

The only medal I ever wanted was the Good Conduct Medal, missed it by sixteen days, just two weeks short of a year, the time needed to behave without blemish before the medal could be awarded. My time as an enlisted man was up; I had a new commitment as a commissioned officer having just graduated from the Infantry School at Benning. Everything started anew. An officer and a gentleman, and officers were ineligible for this award, their conduct expected to be beyond reproach.

I was always accused of misbehavior growing up, a reluctance to accept authority, especially when such authority was governed by tenets of hypocrisy. History was bunk, one lie after another; English was *Silas Marner*; Poli Sci was the virtues of capitalism, never mind the social and economic stratification that it creates. Raised Lutheran, I quarreled with faith superintending good works and disdained the Catholic behavior of friends who were taught theirs was the one true religion, insisting on expostulating that view, blasphemous and heretical from my perspective.

I carried resentment on my shoulders like a sixty-pound pack along with a few hundred rounds of ammunition. Throughout the years, my unassailably realistic assessments were equated with cynicism by colleagues. A dislike of eternally Pollyannaish optimism gave me the moniker *curmudgeon*. I had to live with that characterization for a lifetime, all because I had no proof otherwise, no Good Conduct Medal to affirm my just and accurate appraisal of the world, my honest place in that world. Now, for posterity's sake, there will be no record of good behavior, and all my misdeeds will be celebrated: *Bad to the very marrow of his bone*, my eulogy, my epitaph.

SETTING IT STRAIGHT: A SATIRICAL ESSAY
DESIGNED TO PERSUADE THE UNTHINKING
TO DO THE UNTHINKABLE

No culture, no society, no nation, can tell the truth of its history: indeed, perhaps the greatest spoil of war is the privilege of writing the history, nuance buried, shame and embarrassment nowhere in evidence, a profligate distortion to be taught to subsequent generations. No American history book would state that the war with Japan did not begin on 7 December 1941, but more than a century earlier when gunboat diplomacy insisted Japan open its borders to trade with the West. When children of the American South are taught that the North fired the first shot at Ft. Sumter, they adamantly, vociferously, object to the indisputable, verifiable fact that Abraham Lincoln refused to fire first upon the dissolution of the Union: the deniers are incredulous, asking, "Well, what were Union forces doing there in the South in the first place?" The rejoinder being that it was a federal installation and the States were unified, if in name only, so of course American forces were there in the capacity of federal protection for all. One can only go so far with this argument based upon factual evidence; a barrier exists which allows no penetration. The North, according to Southern mythology, was always the aggressor—hence the Southern appellation for the Civil War as the War of Northern Aggression.

President William Jefferson Clinton frequently addressed the nation on the continual problem of race relations in America, the long, troubled history always a flashpoint, but, to the credit of American politicians, a lot has been done in the past few decades to reduce racial inequality. Democrats, with the support of Joe Biden, passed the Violent Crime Control and Law Enforcement Act of 1994 in an attempt to minimize the impact of the tyranny of the minority. The act created large disparities in sentencing for those convicted of using crack cocaine as opposed to cocaine in its powdered form, thereby incarcerating many more black Americans for what is essentially the same offense as that committed by white Americans. This redressing of a wrong is consistent with traditional American values. For example, President Gerald Ford pardoned Robert E. Lee for his treasonous offense of taking up arms against the government of the United States. Righting wrongs is the American way. As further proof, I offer the recent Florida Board of Education approval of standards that will set our history straight. With these new standards, Florida students will learn how "slaves developed skills which . . . could be applied for their personal benefit." Still, with CRT prohibited in the classroom, the discussion will inevitably continue, CRT being nothing more than a truthful telling of American history, e.g., the Chinese Exclusion Act, the Trail of Tears, the internment of Japanese-Americans, the red-lining of cities, and the displacement of native Hawaiians. Regrettably, this discussion on race will insistently and unnecessarily befuddle future generations, hence an immediate redress of wrongs is warranted. The idea of reparations has been raised previously in the past, but it is now time to put this reparations policy into effect. Along with those personal skills African American slaves were provided, they were also given food, lodging, and a healthy job in a sunny climate that kept them in good, physical shape. In recognition of these benefits—and to put the issue of race behind us once and for all—descendants of those slaves should be billed, as part of the reparations program, for the food, housing, and skills taught them for their personal benefit. Florida is showing the way. Our thoughts and prayers should be with Governor DeSantis and the courageous members of the Florida Board of Education who have shown us the rightful path to enlightenment. All Americans can agree it is time to bury this issue of race, and the program will have the additional benefit of having reparations money to offset the deficit and to clear out all school libraries of books that offer erroneous and upsetting information. When the library shelves are bare, we will achieve a righteous shock of recognition and understanding. Our Constitution guarantees freedom, not the least of which is the freedom not to read anything one does not wish to read. No one should be forced to read, and if it may be argued by those possessed of liberal imaginations that this policy might result in a race of stupid people, those liberal imaginers should be reminded that Donald Trump has said he "loves stupid people." And President Abraham Lincoln famously said that, "God must dearly love stupid people because he made so many of them." Our future generations will be loved by God and Donald Trump, a consummation devoutly to be wished.

D.E. Ritterbusch is the author of several previous collections of poetry including *The Stinger*, *Far from the Temple of Heaven*, and *Lessons Learned: Poetry of the Vietnam War and its Aftermath* based on his military experience as an officer in the U.S. Army. He was twice selected to be the Distinguished Visiting Professor in the Department of English and Fine Arts at the United States Air Force Academy and recently retired after a long career as a Professor of English at the University of Wisconsin-Whitewater. His creative and scholarly work has been archived in the Department of Special Collections on the imaginative representations of the Vietnam War at La Salle University in Philadelphia. He has published hundreds of poems and prose pieces in various periodicals, and his work has been dealt with in various books, articles, conference presentations, and dissertations. He was awarded an $8,000 Wisconsin Arts Board grant for his book *Lessons Learned*. He is a Vietnam veteran with a profound service-connected loss of hearing. His unit was awarded a Meritorious Unit Citation. He lives in his hometown, Waukesha, Wisconsin, and winters in Surprise, Arizona.

Made in the USA
Columbia, SC
17 October 2024

44576181R00061